RIBBONS & TRIMS

PHOTOGRAPHY BY **CLAIRE RICHARDSON**

ANNABEL LEWIS

RIBBONS & TRIMS

POTTER
CRAFT

New York

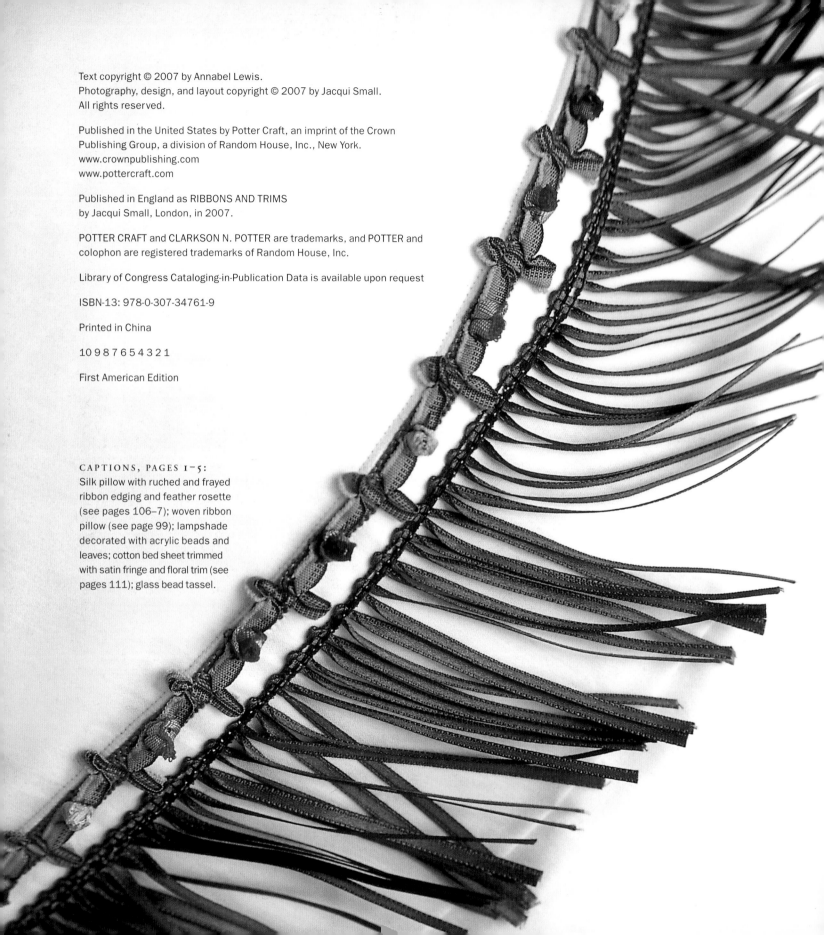

Published in the United States by Potter Craft, an imprint of the Crown
Publishing Group, a division of Random House, Inc., New York.
www.crownpublishing.com
www.pottercraft.com

Published in England as RIBBONS AND TRIMS
by Jacqui Small, London, in 2007.

POTTER CRAFT and CLARKSON N. POTTER are trademarks, and POTTER and
colophon are registered trademarks of Random House, Inc.

Library of Congress Cataloging-in-Publication Data is available upon request

ISBN-13: 978-0-307-34761-9

Printed in China

10 9 8 7 6 5 4 3 2 1

First American Edition

CAPTIONS, PAGES 1–5:
Silk pillow with ruched and frayed
ribbon edging and feather rosette
(see pages 106–7); woven ribbon
pillow (see page 99); lampshade
decorated with acrylic beads and
leaves; cotton bed sheet trimmed
with satin fringe and floral trim (see
pages 111); glass bead tassel.

contents

THIS PAGE I love the tones of shaded ombré ribbon. This beautiful combination of green and mauve makes me think of a butterfly fluttering around lavender, while the silk fabric shimmers and rustles like Marie Antoinette's skirts. There is an old-fashioned feel to the ruching and pleating, which makes this lampshade perfect for an elegant boudoir or genteel tea table (see pages 150–1).

OPPOSITE These silk taffeta curtains are made from uncut ribbon fabric in subtle tones of pale blue and pink on old rose with a sharp lime stripe. The purple tieback is made from semiprecious stones (see similar on pages 120–1).

introduction

As a child I spent a lot of time with my grandmother, mainly cutting out cotton fabrics with a template to make hexagonal patches for patchwork quilts. She had a fantastic sewing box with thimbles, embroidery thread, buttons, scraps of velvet, and satin ribbons. Anything that was reusable would be put into the box. So from a young age I was constantly making things, not only with ribbons but with all manner of materials.

I grew up on a farm in England's "Lake District" and living there in the late 1960s was truly rural. Farming techniques were basic compared with today; instead of complex machinery, you could still find whole rolls of baler twine, used for binding bales of hay, as well as tapes and string. One of my favorite things was the metal whisk-type twister used to close the wire around the top of the jute grain sacks. I would make the wire into jewelry and fashion pillows from the sacking. Feathers were everywhere, and looking for hen's

eggs was a whole day's activity. Our dresses always had pockets, so that's where we put the eggs and feathers we collected. The eggs, colored putty gray, blue, green, and brown, were speckled or blotched, but it is their tones and textures that I remember and which now influence my designs for ribbons and trims. A wire-edged ribbon may be inspired by the color of a pheasant egg, for example—shady gray shot with taupe and blue. The cords and string that I now use professionally also have their roots in these memories. I would spend hours trying to see how the string that held together a paper sack of cattle food was woven. If you have not opened a sack of cattle food, you will never know, but you will find a technique not dissimilar in some of the following projects.

Reinventing outdoor finds for indoors is a challenge I rise to, but the pieces generally need a bit of work. I keep logs by the fire in a decorated tin cattle-food bin and I upholstered

OPPOSITE Always keep a bits-and-pieces box at your elbow. Mine is upholstered in the best colors ever—deep buttoning in brown satin on one side and pale blue on the other, with contrasting satin buttons. It is overflowing with vintage motifs, old trims, and some new pieces, such as the beaded flower, which is ready for me to pick out and stitch onto a lampshade. In the background are old Italian church hangings with a lovely ribbon design in copper and gold.
LEFT These vintage silver metallic tassels adorning an old plinth are an unusual shape—the style of tassel top is referred to as netting and the small skirt is made of twisted bullion. The tie is a traditional mixture of real metal thread and silver yarn.

a garden bench for use indoors (see pages 96–7). You could also wrap an old wine crate with cord and use it to store outdoor shoes, while a trash can covered with fabric and tassels would make a great laundry basket.

With so many materials to choose from, I have no problem coming up with ideas. First comes inspiration for the color, followed by the texture. Then I may invent something to be used as a wall covering or trim, or to create a lampshade or other decorative item that will make an impact. Ribbons and trims can be manipulated easily, so they are perfect for adorning chairs and door panels, and for making carpet edgings and wall decorations. Attaching a new heading to existing fringes and tassels will transform and reinvigorate a piece of furniture, as will wrapping it with ribbon or cord, or adding a braid or pompom. I see an old chair with an appealing shape and imagine it covered with grosgrain ribbon, reinvented by the vibrant color or unusual texture.

If someone asks me where I find inspiration, I say, "In every conceivable thing as well as in some things you may not even conceive." Color grabs me first, or an unusual design. For example, I have a collection of fabric with different birds on each piece. It may only be the swallow's tail or a wren on a leaf with half its tail feathers missing, but to feel and see a ribbon or fabric evolve from these is all I would wish to do all day. Ribbons themselves—in particular, my collection of design documents from the 1840s—have inspired not only more ribbons, but also fabric and furniture designs, as well as lines of rugs and wallpapers. Once, in Paris, I found a vibrant lime- and emerald-green tufted 1940s' ribbon, which was reborn as a mad "Hula Hoop" fabric. The silk ribbon fabrics featured in this book are uncut ribbons. I love these so much that I often keep them as a bolt of fabric, unsliced into strips of taffeta tagliatelle. I jump at the chance to trawl through a flea market or rummage in an old thrift store. I once found an eighteenth-century bodice in lovely peachy tones with a design of coral, which inspired a line of beaded trims to go with the fabric I had reproduced. This waited patiently for its moment to upholster the perfect scallop-shaped chair. As with all partnerships, sometimes you have to wait till the stars are harmoniously aligned for a trim or fabric to find the object it's made for. With 5,000 different trims to choose from at V V Rouleaux, I can design and invent till the cows come home. "Where to start?" is not a question I ever use; it's more "Where will I finish?"

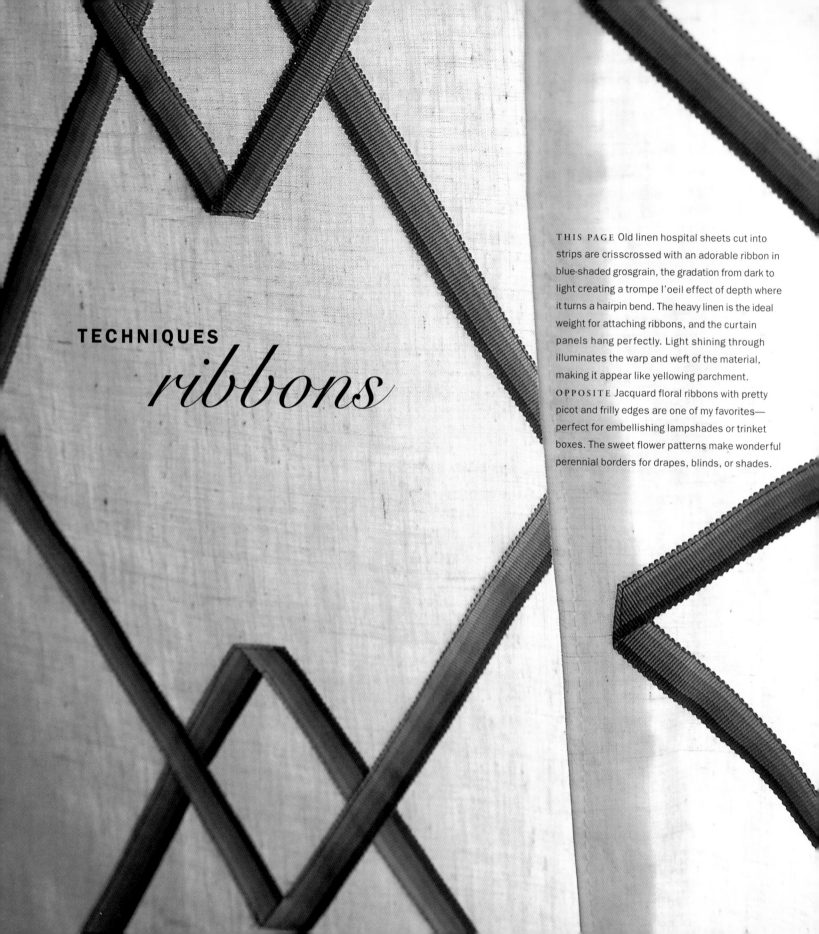

TECHNIQUES
ribbons

THIS PAGE Old linen hospital sheets cut into strips are crisscrossed with an adorable ribbon in blue-shaded grosgrain, the gradation from dark to light creating a trompe l'oeil effect of depth where it turns a hairpin bend. The heavy linen is the ideal weight for attaching ribbons, and the curtain panels hang perfectly. Light shining through illuminates the warp and weft of the material, making it appear like yellowing parchment.
OPPOSITE Jacquard floral ribbons with pretty picot and frilly edges are one of my favorites—perfect for embellishing lampshades or trinket boxes. The sweet flower patterns make wonderful perennial borders for drapes, blinds, or shades.

satin to organdy

A country childhood taught me that beautiful things could also be useful, and I consider all ribbons and trims to be of no value at all unless they have at least five different uses. There are endless colors and types of ribbon—silk, organdy, velvet, grosgrain, jacquard, satin, and wire-edged—many of which originate from something as utilitarian as horse belting or the embellishment on military uniforms.

European countries have a great history of traditional costumes and ribbons play a significant part in this display of patriotism. The French are the leading manufacturers of high-quality wire-edged ribbons—there are as many as 65 solid colors to choose from—but unfortunately there are now very few English manufacturers, and I like to think we have helped the few remaining to continue with this art. Across the globe, the Japanese produce exquisite ribbons and amazing yarn on extraordinary machines, while pure silk ribbon is largely sourced from Asia Pacific. The curtain on page 7 is an example of silk taffeta ribbon fabric before it is cut into individual ribbons. I have also had silk ribbon made by a manufacturer in France, copied from 1840s designs.

There is a long tradition of presenting flowers, chocolates, and gifts tied with beautiful bows, but now ribbons can also be seen in interiors and fashion. Wire-edged ribbon is superb for making simple bows, and you can also use it to make rosebuds, which I attach to lampshades or curtains, or mass together and display in a lovely glass dish. These can be

LEFT The fabric used to upholster this sofa, "Chevron," was inspired by part of one of the ribbons in V V Rouleaux's collection of design documents from the 1840s. These original designs feature a breathtaking array of colors, many in combinations that are so contemporary you can't believe they are from the 1840s. A red feather lampshade and a black feather wall display, influenced by African headdresses but in fact made from a straw plate charger (see pages 48–9), complement the colors in the fabric.
OPPOSITE Strands of picot satin ribbon glued to a bamboo pole hang as a curtain, giving a view to the garden beyond. A charming idea for a child's room, this type of curtain can also keep out insects at an unscreened window or door.

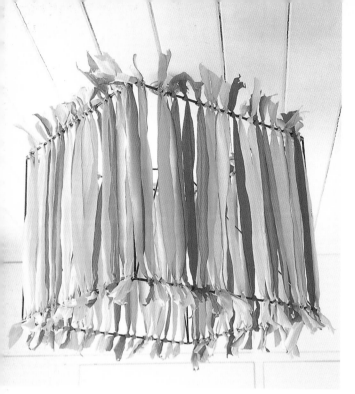

LEFT Colorful wire-edged ribbons knotted at the top and bottom onto a square wire frame make a bright and breezy lampshade for a teenager's room—any shape of shade would work equally well. The ends of the clashing ribbons are cut into a fishtail shape.

OPPOSITE My favorite vintage bedspread features sumptuous French ribbons in green, gold, brown, and orange. To apply this color scheme successfully to the rest of the room, I would tone down the yellow for the walls, cover chairs in orange and taupe, and have curtains in a green silk with pinstripes of dark chocolate, fluorescent yellow, and orange.

BELOW I never throw anything away, and scraps of ribbon and other fabric can be put to good use in covering and trimming old boxes to give them a new lease on life. Ribbons can even be used to hold the lid in place if the hinges have broken. If you pad the lid with a little batting, it makes an ideal place to store brooches or even pins and needles.

solid colors or shaded darker to lighter, and frayed, ruched, pleated, and manipulated to form great blowsy blooms. The wider the width of the ribbon, the larger the rose and vice versa.

One of the most complicated ribbons to make is a cut-pile velvet, which can be of varying qualities in nylon, mixed polyester, or viscose. Old velvet ribbons were made from silk, but these are rare nowadays, as less-expensive viscose and cotton make a very sumptuous sheen. There is an interesting technique for imprinting a design that uses a heat effect to push down the pile. Other ribbon manufacturers have a technique called "sonic cut," which enables the ribbon to take on a lace effect or a scalloped edge. Velvet ribbon, which can be printed, wired, and elasticized, will never lose its appeal; vibrant spring colors have recently become popular, making it a year-round perennial, not merely a winter favorite.

Strong and elegant, grosgrain has a classic ribbed design and is the ribbon used for military uniforms and medals. Traditionally made of cotton and viscose, it is extremely versatile as it will go around corners, so it is often used to trim lampshades, hats, collars, and pockets. Also, in the 1960s and 1970s, when the fashion was for walls to be covered with burlap, 1¼-inch-wide grosgrain in a contrasting color was often used as edging, as well as an embellishment for furniture, curtains, and valances. Grosgrain has two manufacturing processes, one on an old shuttle loom, the other on a fast loom. The former produces the *pièce de résistance* of all chic classic ribbed ribbon, made famous by Coco Chanel and identified by its narrow picot woven edge.

To find a lovely jacquard ribbon is a delight to me. They are usually all traditional designs, as they are made by a special process. The designs are on a punched-card roller system—a roll of patterns to be followed, which the machine processes into the ribbon as it is woven. My main suppliers, in Italy and Germany, produce the most beautiful antique styles. Contemporary patterns are geometric, with dots or varied stitch details.

basic *ribbons*

1 **SINGLE-SIDED VELVET** 1½ inches wide; ideal for weaving, trimming walls and lampshades, and covering coat hangers.

2 **DOUBLE-SIDED VELVET** ¾ inch wide; use for layering, weaving, and trimming and edging pillows and cushions.

3 **PLAIN TAFFETA** 1¾ inches wide; great for wide weaving and trimming walls.

4 **SHOT ORGANDY** 1¾ inches wide; ideal for bows, weaving, wrapping lampshades and making sheer curtains.

5 **GROSGRAIN** 1¾ inches wide; a great robust multipurpose ribbon, especially good for covering furniture.

6 **PICOT SATIN** 1 inch wide; use for hanging curtains and picture bows.

7 **MOIRE TAFFETA** 2 inches wide; great for picture bows and weaving.

8 **WIRE-EDGED** 2 inches wide; perfect for weaving, ruching, fraying, wrapping, and making picture bows and roses.

9 **JACQUARD WIRE-EDGED** 1¾ inches wide; as above.

10 **ORGANDY WITH SATIN EDGE** 2 inches wide; use for bows and embellishments, and for fraying or ruching.

11 **ORGANDY WITH TRANSFER DOT PRINT** 1¾ inches wide; as above.

12 **SATIN** ⅝ inch wide; ideal for weaving or trimming, including walls.

13 **PICOT GROSGRAIN** ¼ inch wide; great for trimming walls, edging lampshades, or making tassel skirts.

14 **STRETCH ORGANDY** ¾ inch wide; use for ties and picture bows.

15 **METALLIC JACQUARD WIRE-EDGED** 1¾ inches wide; great for edging and trimming furniture and walls.

special *ribbons*

1 **PLEATED SATIN** 1 inch wide; use to trim cushions, furniture, and lampshades.

2 **KNITTED WOOL BRAID WITH METALLIC THREAD** ½ inch wide; glue onto furniture, walls, frames, or lampshades.

3 **KNITTED BRAID** ⅝ inch wide; use as above.

4 **LINEN JACQUARD** 1¾ inches wide; ideal for bows and edging pillows.

5 **PLEATED TAFFETA** ⅝ inch wide; use for picture bows and rosettes.

6 **WOVEN JACQUARD WITH SEERSUCKER CENTER** 1½ inches wide; use for walls, edging, and picture bows.

7 **ORGANDY** 3 inches wide; great for weaving, ribbon curtains, and bows.

8 **DENIM STITCH TAPE** ½ inch wide; use for weaving and bows, and for trimming pillow cases, towels, and walls.

9 **LACE** 3½ inches wide; use to trim lampshades or to edge curtains.

10 **SATIN AND ORGANDY STRIPE** ⅝ inch wide; great for weaving and bows, and for trimming lampshades, towels, or pillow cases.

11 **VINTAGE PICOT TAFFETA** 3 inches wide; use for walls, furniture embellishment, or cushions.

12 **BOX-PLEAT STRIPE SATIN** ⅝ inch wide; use to make picture bows and to trim furniture, lampshades, and bed linen.

13 **LINEN WITH JACQUARD DESIGN** 4 inches wide; use to trim walls, cushions, and bedspreads.

14 **PLEATED ORGANDY** 1½ inches wide; use for lampshades and bows.

15 **FLOWER POM TAPE KNITTED AND HAND-STITCHED** use to trim lampshades, cushions, and chairs.

16 **TRANSFER DOT PRINT GROSGRAIN** ¾ inch wide; good for trimming walls, furniture, and cushions, and for bows and weaving.

17 **TAFFETA WITH COLORED EDGE** ¼ inch wide; ideal for weaving and trimming.

18 **HAND-EMBROIDERED VELVET** 1¼ inches wide; use for bows and to trim lampshades, frames, and pillows.

technique ribbon basics

Ribbons are easy to manipulate, but each type of ribbon has its optimum use. Wire-edged ribbons can be ruched, frayed, and folded; grosgrain lends itself to being glued onto furniture; satin is flimsy, making it suitable for weaving and stitching onto other fabrics; organdy can be stitched and ruched, and is great for window treatments, thanks to its sheer quality.

CUTTING RIBBON

There are several ways to cut the ends of a ribbon to prevent it from fraying, depending on the decorative effect you wish to achieve and the intended use of the ribbon.

DECORATIVE CUTS The best way to cut narrow ribbon is to snip the end diagonally. If the ribbon is wide, fold the end in half lengthwise and make a diagonal cut across the fold, toward the center of the ribbon, to create a fishtail shape. Use the same method to make multiple cuts, folding the ribbon back and forth on itself like an accordion and cutting across the fold to create a shark's tooth or zigzag pattern. This is best done on tightly woven wire-edged ribbon or ribbon wider than 1 inch, but you can also make this type of cut along the length of a ribbon folded back and forth on itself. This is known as a pleated cut and is great for creating a decorative edging.

FRAYING RIBBON

A lovely decorative effect can be created by fraying ribbon along its length, either on one edge only or along both edges. This looks fantastic on shot ribbon, which is woven with two colors, as you will get threads of both colors in the fringe. Use this for trimming or decorating everything from furniture and cushions to curtains and lampshades.

1 Take a piece of wire-edged ribbon and cut off one of the long edges.

2 Carefully pull the vertical threads away to make a frayed edge.

3 When you have removed enough threads to create the depth of frayed fringe you require, sew a small zigzag stitch along the edge of the ribbon at this point to prevent the fabric from fraying beyond this line of stitching.

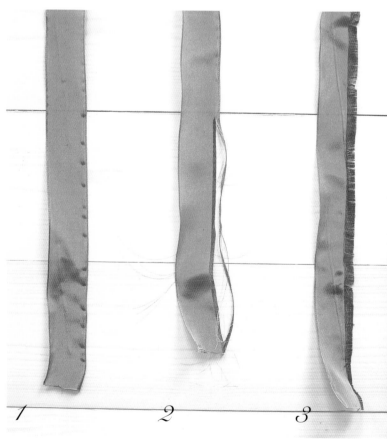

1   *2*   *3*

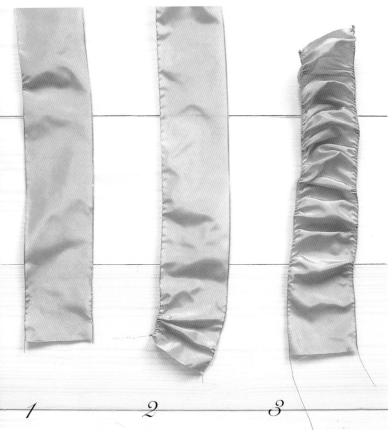

RUCHING WIRE-EDGED RIBBON

Also known as gathering, ruching can be achieved by pulling the wires on both edges of a wire-edged ribbon. Gathering only one edge creates a circular shape, which is used to make a ribbon rose (see page 22). A ribbon gathered along both edges is one of my favorite ways to cover nails and upholstery tacks. It will go easily around corners if you ruche the ribbon more on one side than the other, and can be manipulated in many ways for various decorative applications. Ribbons in plain designs work best for this technique, especially if they are lightweight, as the ruching would hide a pattern.

1 Take a length of wire-edged ribbon. You will need a piece at least twice as long as the finished length you intend to end up with, to allow for the ruching. Pull out about ½ inch of wire on both edges at one end of the ribbon and secure by bending the wires backwards or poking the ends through the ribbon.

2 Go to the other end of the ribbon and pull out the ends of both wires. Holding these firmly, push the ribbon fabric evenly toward the secure end.

3 Keep pulling the wires, making sure they are level, and pushing the ribbon fabric into a ruche. Secure the wires by winding them around each end or by poking them through the ribbon.

RUCHING RIBBON WITH THREAD

It is also possible to gather or ruche ribbon that does not have wire edges by stitching one or more lines of gathering stitch along the length of the ribbon, either at the edge or in the center, and then pulling the thread in the same way as you would wire, as described above. You can either use a single ribbon or layered ribbons placed on top of each other to create a full ruffle. Follow the methods below.

1 To ruche a ribbon centrally, use a needle and matching thread to sew a line of running stitch lengthwise down the middle of the ribbon—draw a guideline with tailor's chalk first if you need to. Gently pull the thread to create a ruche, easing the ribbon fabric into even gathers along its length and being careful not to break the thread.

2 To create a ribbon frill, use a needle and matching thread to sew a line of running stitch along one edge of the ribbon and pull the thread gently to gather the ribbon fabric along its length.

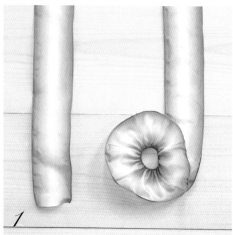
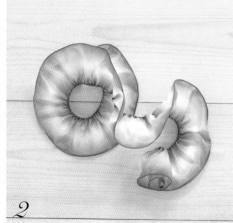

RIBBON ROSES

You can make tight rosebuds with very narrow wire-edged ribbon, or use wide ribbon to create big voluptuous blooms that could almost hold their own at flower shows. They can be plain solid colors or shaded or shot through with another color. I sew them to lampshades, curtains, or scatter cushions, or simply display a selection of bright clashing blooms in a glass bowl. I like to mix the colors—acid yellow next to purple and vibrant orange in contrast with pale green and dusky pink. As well as color, proportion plays its part, so arrange soft sugar pink and fuchsia mini-buds among bigger blooms—all shades, shapes, and sizes jostling for space together.

1 Pull out ½ inch of wire from one edge of the ribbon at one end and secure. Pull the other end of that wire, gathering the ribbon along one edge only to create a circular shape.

2 Tightly roll up one end of the ruched side of the ribbon to create the bud at the center of the rose. Continue rolling, and as your flower gets bigger, move the next fold outward, farther away from the center. Adjust the flower shape as necessary and pin as you go.

3 Using a needle and thread, sew the ribbon on the reverse of the flower shape to hold it in position. Make sure you sew the center securely so the bud doesn't fall out of the middle of the coil.

ROSETTE

This is a traditional decoration for giftwrapping, often mass produced in a poor-quality plastic ribbon. Here is its stylish cousin, made from a gorgeous lime grosgrain, the texture of which helps each petal to hold its shape. Tie it to a key on a closet door or use to adorn a picture frame.

1 For each "leaf" shape, cut a piece of ribbon 4 inches long and fold it over, crossing the ends as shown below, and pin in place. Make as many leaves as you need in the same way, depending on how large you want your finished rosette to be.

2 Place all the leaf shapes in a circular design, overlapping them a little, and pin then stitch them together. For the tails of the rosette, cut a piece of ribbon 6 inches long, fold it in half and sew it onto the back of the rosette.

3 To finish, sew running stitch lengthwise down the center of a piece of ribbon 12 inches long and pull the thread to ruche the ribbon, then sew this to the center of the rosette.

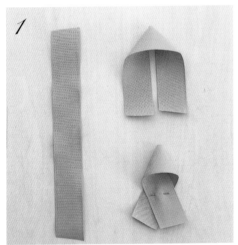

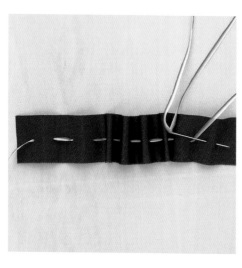

SEWING WITH RIBBON

Plain purple grosgrain ribbons have been decorated with simple running stitch using a narrow blue ombré ribbon, then sewn parallel to each other onto a pillow cover.

THREADED RIBBON Cut 2-inch-wide grosgrain ribbon into lengths of 20 inches (or the width of your pillow). Find a pointed needle with a large eye, such as a sharps needle, thread it with 20 inches of thin lightweight but strong ribbon and make a knot in the end. Sew random but fairly large basting stitches centrally through the lengths of grosgrain ribbon. Finish with a knot on the underside, as you would if you were sewing with thread.

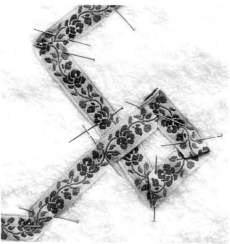

RIBBON PLEATING

Plain towels have been transformed with the addition of a pretty jacquard flower-patterned ribbon and blue woven and striped designs. For this technique, which works equally well on sheets and curtains, you need a double-sided ribbon—or one with an interesting reverse side. A ribbon with a tight weave, which is not too slippery, will be easiest to work with and will keep its shape better when manipulated into folds.

FOLDING OR PLEATING RIBBON Decide on your design and draw it to scale on paper. Working on a flat surface, place the ribbon on the fabric and pin in place, following the pattern, then baste and sew by hand or with a sewing machine.

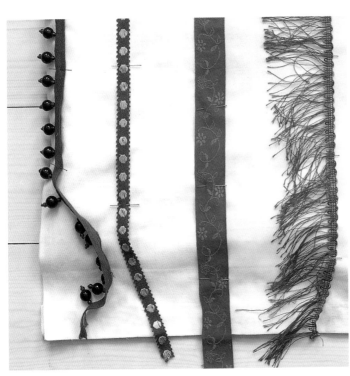

ATTACHING RIBBON TRIM

Trims are usually attached horizontally—either sewn in place or secured with glue. A variety of different ribbons and trims in harmonizing colors can make a great visual impact when attached vertically to plain white curtain panels. Glass bead trim, fringes, floral tape, and a mixture of ribbons have been massed together to stunning effect.

SEWING RIBBONS When trimming curtains or bed linen with ribbon, sewing is the best method. For a seamless finish, use single pieces of ribbon the same length as the fabric you are trimming. Measure regular intervals across the width of the fabric to make sure each piece of ribbon is spaced evenly. Decide on the order of trimmings and pin each one in place, making sure it is straight. Turn the ends under for a neat finish at the top and bottom edges and sew in place with a needle and matching thread.

WRAPPING WITH RIBBON

Using ribbons to cover objects is a simple technique that is especially useful for concealing a plain or ugly form or texture. It doesn't matter what shape the object is, because you can overlay and manipulate the ribbon to fit it as you wrap. You can layer the ribbon either randomly or precisely, butting up each piece side by side for a smooth finish.

An example of this technique used to great effect is these plain pine bedposts, which have been covered with ⅝-inch-wide ribbons in subtle tones of putty gray, taupe, and shades of blue to make a marvelous vertical stripe. The headboard is made from woven ribbon in wider stripes of the same colors, while the pale blue bedspread is decorated with pretty tufts of ribbon (see page 40).

1 Measure the surface to be covered and cut lengths of ribbon to fit exactly, edge to edge. You may need to use a combination of widths to achieve a perfect fit. Stick double-sided tape onto the surface and remove the backing. Take your first piece of ribbon and carefully lay it flush with the edge of the post and smooth it down, making sure there are no wrinkles or creases.

2 Build up the stripe by adding more double-sided tape and more strips of ribbon in the same way, until the post is completely covered. Add the ribbons one at a time and butt each one up flush with the previous strip.

3 For a neat finish, trim off any overlapping ends of ribbon if necessary. Then cut a piece of felt in a harmonizing color to the exact size of the top of the bedpost and stick it in place using glue or double-sided tape as before.

1

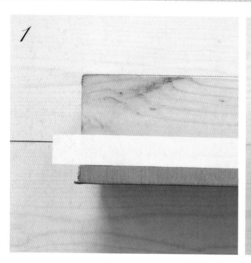

2

3

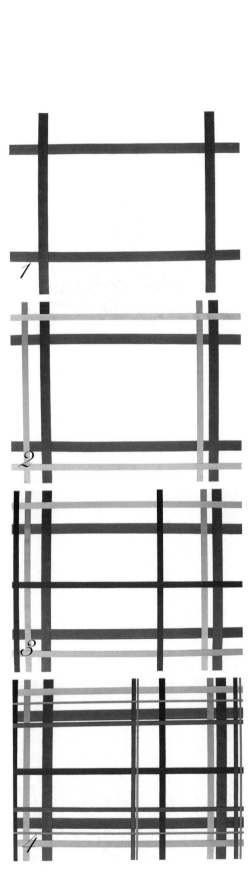

LAYERING TO CREATE A PLAID PATTERN

Tartan plaid doesn't have to be the traditional heavy reds, greens, and blues—it can be subtle or bold and contemporary, and works well on a small or large scale. I'm sure there is a certain way plaid should be created, but I like to take a more relaxed approach, building up the pattern with large and smaller squares in various widths and colors to create an open effect. Just play around and see what works. The most important thing is to choose colors that look good together and that will cross over well, such as moss green with plum and gold, with a bright pink to make that square of the layered plaid stand out.

1 After you've chosen your ribbons, measure and mark a basic grid on the area you wish to cover. If you are working on a large area, such as a wall, use a carpenter's level and plumb line to make sure your grid is straight. For a permanent finish, use PVA glue to hold the ribbon in place; otherwise, used double-sided tape. Start with the widest ribbon and apply the two horizontal lines first, then smooth the vertical lines in place.

2 Using a narrower ribbon in a contrasting color, create a second grid in the same formation, but just outside and to the left of the original grid.

3 Create an irregular grid using a third ribbon, filling in the large square by placing this grid farther away from the original grid.

4 Continue building up the pattern as you wish, but make sure you add at least one contrasting color to make the pattern pop out.

LAYERED RIBBON PANEL

The simplest way to join several lengths of ribbon together is by using iron-on interfacing. This allows you to layer ribbons of various colors, textures, and widths quickly and easily to create a single piece of fabric that can be used to cover anything from chair seats to cushion covers. You can make this piece of fabric as small or as large as you wish by adding more lengths of ribbon. Just make sure that the interfacing you choose is of a strong enough quality for however you intend to use it.

USING IRON-ON INTERFACING TO CREATE A PANEL Make a selection of ribbons in various colors and widths, and cut them to the required length. Pin the ribbons vertically side by side to a soft board, with right sides facing down. Make sure the lengths of ribbon are straight and that they butt up to each other with no gaps between, and secure with pins at both ends. Lay the iron-on interfacing on top and press with an iron according to the manufacturer's instructions.

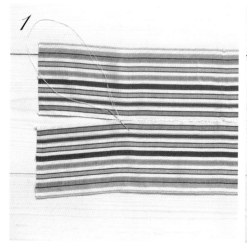

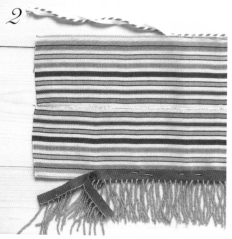

STITCHING A RIBBON PANEL

If you can't find a piece of ribbon wide enough for your intended use, such as upholstering the base of a chair, as shown here, you can easily join two or more pieces together with neat stitches.

1 Measure and cut two pieces of ribbon long enough to go around the base of the chair. Line up the two pieces with right sides facing down and sew them together with a neat slipstitch, keeping the stitches as small and discreet as possible.

2 Pin and then sew a bead fringe to the bottom edge of the ribbon panel. I have doubled up the fringe to make it thicker and added a small piping tape to the top edge for a neat, professional finish.

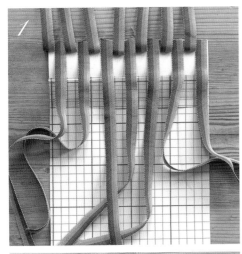

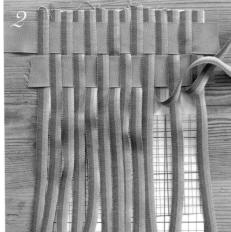

WEAVING ON SELF-ADHESIVE BOARD

This is a simple but effective technique in which vertical ribbons are attached at the top edge and horizontal ribbons are threaded through them, under one and over the next. Using a stiff backing, such as self-adhesive board, will create a fairly rigid woven panel that can be inserted into the panel of a door, for example (see page 152).

1 Cut a piece of self-adhesive board to the correct size for your project—this one fits neatly inside a door panel. Think carefully about the width of ribbon you use, as the strips, when aligned along the top edge, need to fit your piece of cut board exactly. Peel back 2 inches of plastic film and stick down your vertical ribbons side by side with no gaps between them, then lift up alternate ribbons.

2 Begin weaving by laying the first horizontal ribbon on top of the stuck-down vertical ribbons, just beneath the fold of the turned-back ribbons. Fold the vertical ribbons down and lift up the adjacent vertical ribbons, then add another horizontal ribbon.

3 Repeat this process until the card is covered with woven ribbons. Glue it into the door panel and, once it is in place, stick a length of ribbon along the bottom edge.

4 Glue ribbon along the other three outer edges to conceal the joins and finish neatly.

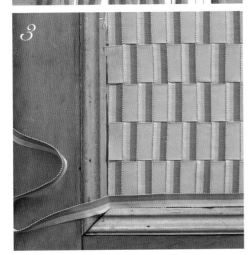

BACKING A WEAVE WITH IRON-ON INTERFACING

To create a woven fabric that is flexible enough to be made into a pillow cover, for example, iron-on interfacing can be used instead of self-adhesive board.

CREATING WOVEN FABRIC Follow the weaving method described on page 29, but begin by pinning the vertical row of ribbons, right sides facing down, onto a soft board. Lift up and fold back alternate ribbons, as before, and pin the horizontal ribbons in place as you go. When you have finished weaving, lay the iron-on interfacing over the woven ribbons and iron according to the manufacturer's instructions.

WEAVING WITHOUT A BACKING

The half-woven organdy curtain above, which is layered over a tulle curtain decorated with ribbon "spiders" (see pages 118–19), is created following the basic weaving method described on page 29. However, instead of using a backing to hold the woven ribbons in place, a decorative stitch is made in each corner where the horizontal and vertical ribbons meet (see opposite). The curtain panel is woven only part of the way down, with the remaining vertical ribbons hanging loose. Made with fine organdy, the curtain is sheer and allows the light to flood through, but you could easily use satin ribbons for a less translucent window treatment. Pretty tablecloths can also be made by this technique.

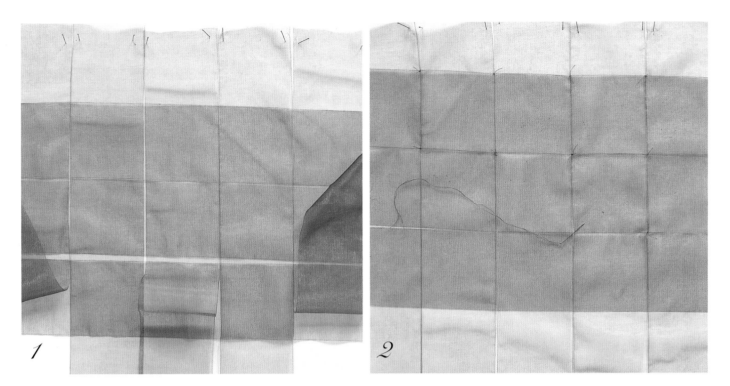

1 First cut pieces of organdy ribbon to the required length—see page 20 for ways to cut the ends of the ribbons so they won't fray. Pin the ribbons to a soft board, side by side in vertical strips, and fold back alternate lengths. Lay the first horizontal piece over the vertical ribbons and pin it in place. You may find it helps to pin each corner, where the ribbons cross each other, as you work. Repeat the process until you have created enough woven fabric for your curtain panel or tablecloth. When creating a large piece of woven fabric, you may find it easier to build up the panel in stages if you are working on a board; alternatively, work against a wall or the floor, holding the ribbon in place with double-sided tape instead of pins.

2 Make sure the ribbons butt up to each other, are straight, and cross over each other at true right angles. Then, either using matching thread or, as here, embroidery thread in a complementary color, sew a neat basting stitch at each corner to join the ribbons. Knot the thread twice on the reverse side of the fabric and cut off the ends. Don't forget to sew the sides of the panel where the vertical and horizontal ribbons meet.

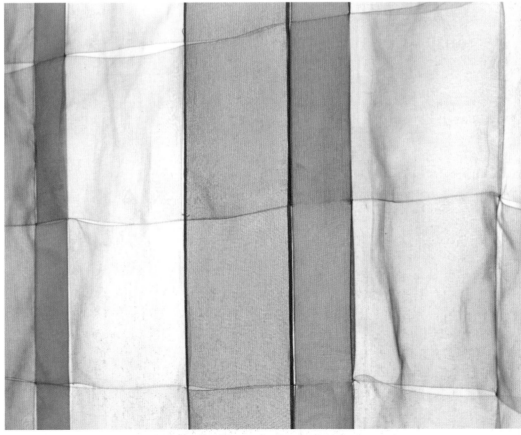

TECHNIQUES
cords & trims

waxed cord
to bullion

Trims can be anything—from string, cord, or fringe (long cut yarn) to pretty floral tape or decorative braid with tassels, beads, or glass drops. Many types of cord that can be put to good use around the home can be found in quite unexpected places and not all are as decorative as those traditionally used for trimming furniture and cushions. Hardware stores have all kinds of string, ropes, and cords in bold bright colors.

PREVIOUS PAGE, LEFT
Chandelier glass is one of my most inspirational objects, conjuring up imaginary rooms tinkling with faceted rounds, pear drops, and icicles. You can hand-sew individual drops to plain braid or buy faux-glass trim made from shaped acrylic. This is much lighter than the real thing and adds instant glamour to an antique sofa.
PREVIOUS PAGE, RIGHT
Versatile turban-style knots can be used for finishing loose ends or as decorative objects in their own right (see pages 46–7). These napkin rings have been made from gold cord fashioned into turban-style knots, with white linen napkins slipped through the center. The gold tassels add extra glamour.

Marine suppliers also have a marvelous variety of ropes that can be cut to any length you require. These types of utilitarian cord do not rot and so can be used outside. You can instantly give garden furniture a new look with huge knots of cord, or nail colorful rope around a tired old wooden table. Garden sheds, barns, and summerhouses can be trimmed with lengths of fat cord around the door or window frames, or wrapped around pillars. Very thick cords make huge turban-style knots that can be used to top a post or as a centerpiece for an outdoor table setting, perhaps holding a chunky altar candle. You could even make your gateposts or tree trunks more festive with colorful cord for a special occasion.

Ordinary string can be drafted into use and knotted, tufted, tasseled, or braided and made into frogging (see page 51) or manipulated into a figure-eight braid and used to edge seats and decorate cushions for a rustic—and economical—outdoor display (see page 44). In addition to the most utilitarian string and cord, there is also a wide choice of decorative trims available that can be used in many ways in the home.

Waxed cord has a great texture and comes in a variety of strong contemporary colors in several widths, making it an ideal choice for covering an object for a bold new look. Like all cords, it can be glued or wired and is versatile because it is so malleable, bending and shaping to whatever you want to cover. Table legs are easy to wrap with waxed cord, or try it on a chandelier or

OPPOSITE Lovely old leather luggage makes the perfect showcase for an array of different tassels, all of which have a turban-style knot as the base and starting point. Knots can be made out of any cord and its thickness is what determines the size of the knot. Once you have your knot, then the possibilities for "skirts," as they are called, is endless— feathers or looped ribbons, as here, or bead or silk fringe, perhaps.

RIGHT I love to reinvent anything I can think of a use for, and these old chimney pots are just the right shape to hold umbrellas, canes, fishing rods, and such like. I simply wrapped them with ⅝-inch-thick cord, sticking it in place using quick-drying glue and a glue gun.

lamp stand that you're bored with (see pages 142 and 146). Furniture and household objects can't afford to become complacent—they need to reinvent themselves (with your help) to keep the love affair fresh. Even items such as picture frames need to keep up with the game—wrap them in lengths and layers for an instant update (see pages 136–7 for ideas).

Flange cord has an edge that can be stitched into a seam and is great for the leading edge of a curtain, as are feather fringes, which could also adorn the lampshades to pull the room scheme—as well as the curtains—together.

Pompom fringes, usually used to trim lampshades or to edge curtains or pillows, can be used in abundance to give a very different look. Try covering a whole pillow or lampshade (see page 146) or even a headboard with pompom fringe.

Traditionally used as a fringe on the base of sofas, bullion is available in an endless choice of colors. In the 1970s it was popular on swags and tails, both of which seem dated now. I think bullion can be used in much more interesting ways, such as the doorstops on pages 52–3 or the pillow cover on page 104, which was inspired by the breed of dog with a very similar chocolate-brown coat. You could also make curtain valances from bullion hung straight across the top, or use it on the backs of dining chairs; place it along the top of the chair back, with a striped grosgrain attached vertically.

I love to give old things a fresh new use, so I'm constantly bringing objects into the house and looking for ways to make them pretty as well as useful. I find all types of cord to be a practical means of covering unsightly items and turning them into stylish interior pieces. Consequently, in addition to various old tables and benches, I have a tin cattle-food bin trimmed with cord, which is used to store logs, battered leather trunks decorated with tassels and turban-style knots (see opposite), and old chimney pots wrapped with cord that make fabulous holders for canes and umbrellas (see above). When you come across a household container, imagine how it might be used. I love to throw anything lying around into the right shaped receptacle; in my book, that means it's neat and out of the way—just don't open any of the closets!

cords & trims

1 **SILVER METALLIC LOOP FRINGE** use to trim cushions or lampshades.

2 **MOCK SUEDE LACE-CUT TAPE** layer on other trims or sew on pillows.

3 **BEADED GLASS TRIM** use on lampshades, pillows, the leading edge of curtains, or hang from a chandelier.

4 **MOCK SNAKE LEATHER** great for wrapping lamp bases.

5 **JACQUARD SILVER METALLIC BRAID** use to edge walls or lampshades.

6 **TWISTED METALLIC CORD** use to decorate pictures or edge walls.

7 **WAXED CORD** use this for wrapping items and making turban-style knots.

8 **KNITTED BRAID** good for edging furniture, walls, and frames.

9 **SCROLL GIMP** use to trim furniture and lampshades, or glue to a lamp stand.

10 **JUTE STRING** use to make tassels, tufts, and turban-style knots.

11 **CHENILLE CORD** great for cushion corners and for edging furniture.

12 **SUEDE TAPE** ideal for layering, edging furniture, or covering hangers.

13 **BRAIDED SUEDE CORD** use as edging or to make turban-style knots.

14 **TWISTED SILKY CORD** use for walling, knots, or frogging.

15 **JUMBO SILVER METALLIC CORD** great edging for walls or furniture.

16 **WAXED MOCK-LEATHER CORD** ideal for turban-style knots and frogging.

17 **TWISTED CORD** as above.

18 **METALLIC JACQUARD BRAID** use to edge walls, frames, or blinds.

19 **FLANGE CORD** use to trim cushions or to edge furniture.

20 **BRAIDED FLANGE CORD** as above.

21 **DYED JUTE GARDEN STRING** use for braiding, knotting, and making tassels and tufts.

22 **FLAT WAXED CORD** great for knotting, wrapping, braiding, and edging walls.

23 **LARGE SISAL CORD** ideal for decorating outdoors: wrapping chairs and framing doors.

technique cord basics

Cord is simple and versatile to work with, as it can be easily manipulated to turn corners and fit the contours and curves of different-shaped objects. It can be wired, sewn, or glued to a surface, as well as being knotted in various ways or used to make tassels and tufts. The most important technique when working with cord is how to cut it to prevent it from fraying.

CUTTING CORDS & TRIMS

Whereas there are several ways to cut the ends of ribbons to prevent them from fraying, both decorative as well as functional (see page 20), there are only two options to prevent cut cords from fraying—binding the end with tape or dipping it in clear glue.

PREVENTING CUT ENDS FROM UNRAVELLING It is essential to use very sharp scissors to cut woven braids and cords, as this will give the cleanest cut. Wrap a piece of clear adhesive tape around the point where you intend to cut the cord and snip straight through the center of the tape—you will end up with a narrow piece of tape wrapped around both newly cut ends. Alternatively, cut the cord cleanly and dip the very end in PVA glue to seal the fibers, then allow to dry.

WIRING CORD

One way of attaching cord to another object is to wrap a length of florist's wire around the end. Once secured around the cord, the ends of the wire can then be twisted around another object or pushed through it and twisted on the inside or reverse.

1 To attach wire to the end of a piece of cord, wrap it around the cord approximately ¼ inch from the cut end and twist the wire firmly three times, so the wire tightens securely around the cord.

2 You can also wire a length of cord by placing a fine wire inside the grooves of the twisted cord, following the twists and firmly pressing the wire into the grooves to conceal it.

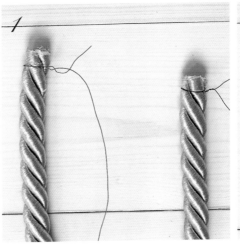

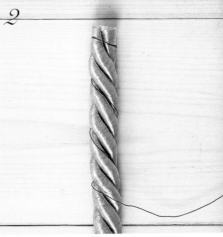

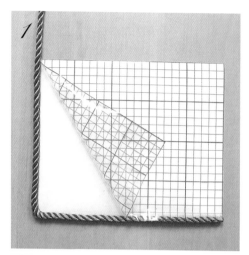

MAKING A PLACE MAT WITH SELF-ADHESIVE BOARD

It's so easy to make place mats from lengths of cord coiled around and around and held in place on a self-adhesive board. The place mats can be any shape and size—round, square, or rectangular—and you can create different looks depending on the type, color, and width of cord you use. If you are making a circular place mat, start in the exact center and work outward; for a square or rectangular place mat, see the steps below.

1 Cut a piece of self-adhesive board into your chosen size and shape and peel back the plastic. Bind the end of the cord in tape and, starting at one side, lay the cord flush along the bottom edge of the board. Work the cord around the corner and up the side.

2 Continue filling in the board, making sure there are no gaps between each layer of cord. Press the cord firmly onto the board where it turns a corner.

3 When you reach the center of the board, bind the cord with tape before cutting it (see page 37), then press the end down firmly.

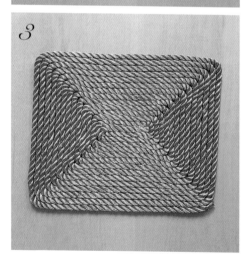

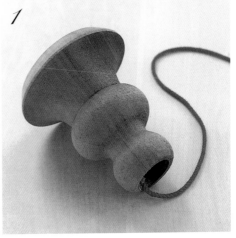

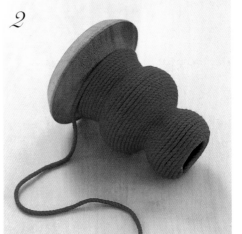

GLUING CORD

Many items can be completely transformed by wrapping them in cord of different widths and colors. Plain curtain finials, which come in lots of shapes and sizes, can be customized with cord to tie in with any interior scheme. Door knobs and newel posts can be treated in a similar way for a very individual look.

1 Using a hot glue gun, stick one end of cord to the inside edge of the wooden mold.

2 Wind the cord around the finial, layering the coils tightly side by side with no gaps, and gluing it in place as you go.

3 Continue to the end of the finial, coiling the cord in decreasing circles until you reach the center point. Cut the end, dip it in PVA, and glue firmly in the center.

TUFTS

These are very versatile decorative knots that can be used in many ways, such as on the al fresco chair seats on page 44 and on the bedspread on the grosgrain-covered four-poster bed on page 26. Tufts can be made from any yarn, including raffia, string, cord, or ribbon, and are formed from a continuous loop tied in the middle. Made with soft yarn, they are perfect for decorating cushions or pillows.

1 For tufts about 3 inches long, you will need approximately 2 yards of ¼-inch-wide ribbon. Wind the ribbon in a figure-eight shape around your finger and thumb 6–7 times, holding them about 3 inches apart.

2 Tie a 3-inch-length of ribbon around the center of the loop with a secure double knot. Cut the ends of the loop and sew the tuft in place, stitching through the back of the knot.

TASSELS

Once you have learned this technique, you will be making tassels out of any form of string, silk, cord, raffia, wool, the works. The tassels illustrated on page 41 are made of garden string and a bargain yarn, so go for it— make hundreds—until you've got the knack and are giving demonstrations to your friends.

Once you've mastered the simple folded top, move on to become the mistress of the turban-style knot (as shown on pages 46–7). Pop one of these over the top of your elementary version and you have the most covetable—and bottom-of-handbag-findable—key ring. To make such a utilitarian object, handled daily, a wonderfully tactile talisman, make the tassel from silky yarn, soft wool, or even strips of buttery leather. I make mine really fat, the better to put my hand on them easily. And why not hang a tassel on the outside of your handbag, too, reclaiming your latest must-have from the herd with a spark of individuality?

Make mini-tassels, 2 inches long, for the corners of a pillow, then make some giant ones to hang from and hold back your curtains—go to extremes. Put one on the end of a light pull cord or attach a few small silky tassels to another larger tassel, as on page 48. Alternatively, hang tassels from chair backs, make jute ones to adorn baskets, and even attach one to the end of an umbrella pull (as on page 44), in case you need to make a quick grab for it on a windy day.

NOTE To help you make the tassel, bang a nail into a block of wood and clamp it securely to the edge of a table.

1 Cut a length of garden string 1 yard long. Fold it in half and make a knot 4 inches in from the top to create a loop and two "legs." Cut another piece of cord 1 yard long.

2 Make a knot and a smaller loop at one end of the second piece of cord—this is so you can secure it onto the nail for tying the neck of the tassel. Then cut 35 lengths of cord 16 inches long. These will together form your tassel.

3 Take the cord with the loop and "legs" and place the loop over the nail. Hold it in your left hand and place the 35 lengths of cord centrally between the legs of cord, below the knot. Tie the "legs" in a tight double knot around these lengths.

4 Fold the 35 pieces in half around the double knot, smoothing the lengths down and making sure the knot is hidden inside the loose ends. Hold this in your left hand, positioning your index finger and thumb at the point where you are going to bind the neck of the tassel. Place the smaller loop over the nail and hold the end of this cord in your right hand.

5 Pass this cord along the inside of the three fingers of your left hand and around the back of your fingers, then flick it from right to left over the top of the tassel, just above your finger and thumb. This is approximately 1 inch below the top knot.

6 Retrieve the cord and pass it 3–4 more times around the neck of the tassel. Each turn of the cord should be just above the previous one. Make sure you catch in the cord from the nail as you wrap.

7 Now pass the cord up through the loop on your three fingers and flick it to the left again and over the top of the tassel.

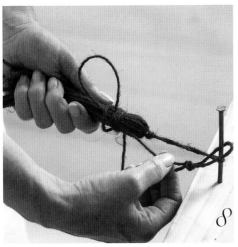

8 Take the loop off your three fingers. Now pull the cord that is attached to the nail away from you and toward the nail. This will catch in your wrapping at the neck of the tassel as you pull tightly. Take the two loose ends of cord and knot them together.

9 Take the tassel off the nail and trim the bottom or, as we call it in the trade, the "skirt," so all the strands are the same length.

OPPOSITE Some of these old folding chairs are missing wooden slats, so to make them more comfy I made padded seats with red string tufts on the deep buttoning and red string tassels on the backs. The table is covered with burlap jute fabric scattered with red beads. A willow trellis—really for training plants like sweet peas—makes a very good place mat. turban-style knots make fun decorations for the umbrella.

THIS PAGE Here is a wonderful variety of turban-style knots in cords of many different textures. The size of the cord determines the size of the knot: ¼-inch-thick twisted cord makes a knot about 1¼ inches in diameter; a jumbo ¾-inch-thick cord would give a knot approximately 8 inches in diameter—great for a finial.

TURBAN-STYLE KNOT

This is one of the most versatile decorative knots, for which you can find endless uses—and making them is great therapy, too. Once you have mastered the technique, your hands will never be idle again. There are so many types of yarns and cords in different weights and textures that you'll never tire of making new knots and finding different places to put them. They are a chic way to finish loose ends, making them ideal for curtain tiebacks (see page 55). They can also be used to top off chic tassels (see pages 48–9) and if you construct the knot loosely, you can insert bead fringe, ribbons, or feathers (see page 34). Several knots can be attached around the rim of a lampshade or umbrella (see page 44), or around the edge of a tablecloth to weigh it down on a blustery day. Make your knot at one end of an extra-long piece of cord, leaving the long cord hanging outside the knot, and this can become a light pull cord. Similarly, with a length of silky cord emerging from a turban-style knot, you have a beautiful decoration for the back of a chair—add another knot to the other end of the cord, tie it in a bow, and let the ends swing.

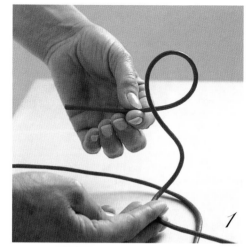

1

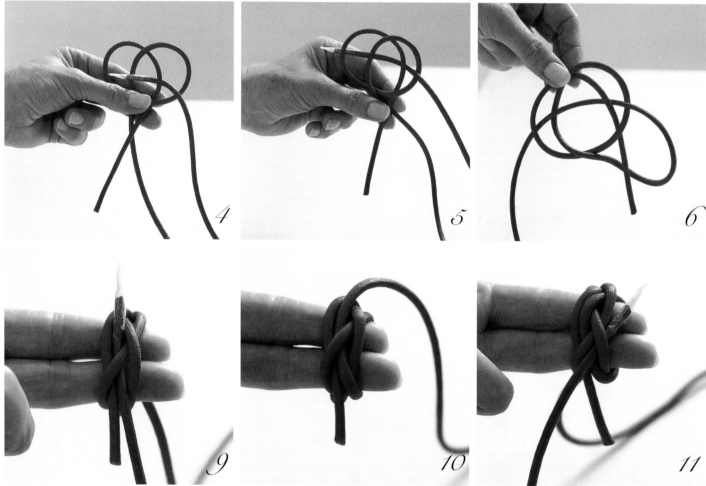

4

5

6

9

10

11

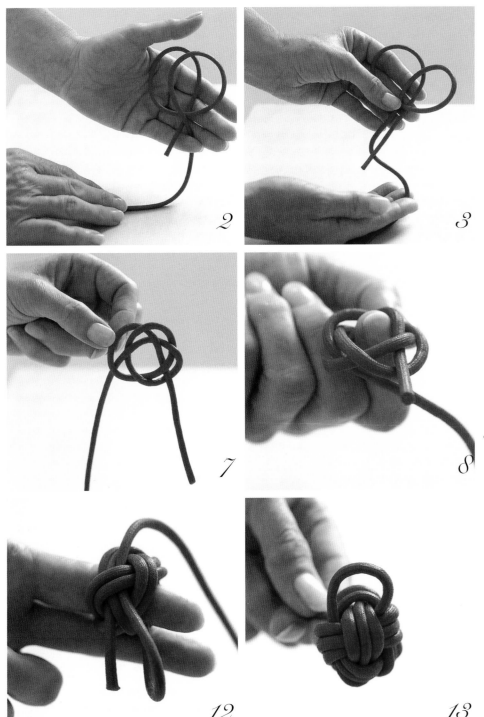

1 Cut a piece of waxed cord 1 yard long. Wrap a lot of clear tape around one end, making it into a point.

2 Starting with the untaped end, make a small loop about 1¼ inches to the left, so the long end passes over the short end. Make another loop on top of the first, overlapping it so there are three holes and two loops.

3 Pass the long end of cord behind the short end.

4 Pass the long taped end through the right-hand loop, front to back, then out through the center hole to the front.

5 Then pass the taped end from front to back through the left loop.

6 Pull the cord all the way through. You will now have something that resembles a pretzel or carpet beater.

7 Pull both cords to make the whole thing smaller.

8 Push the center upward, creating a "wheel," with the short end poking out.

9 Holding this shape on your two first fingers, take the taped end and insert it where the short end is coming out.

10 Pull through and over your fingers.

11 Follow the pattern of the cord, inserting the taped end alongside the single cord. It will first go under the cord, then over the next, building up the shape.

12 Keep following the same cord, side by side, turning the "wheel" as you go. First there will be two cords side by side, then when you meet the short cord again, you will be adding a third cord side by side.

13 This takes a little pushing and pulling, and you will need to manipulate the knot as you work around it to fill it in. You should end up with a hole at the base of the knot, and the taped end will end up inside the hollow center.

MATERIALS

1 straw charger or place mat, 13-inch diameter

Black spray paint

1¼ yards of turkey-feather fringe, 8 inches deep

1¼ yards of ¾-inch-wide black grosgrain ribbon

Glue and glue gun

12 inches florist's wire

2 glass beads, 1-inch diameter

14 inches silky black fringe, 8 inches deep

Narrow-gauge craft or jewelry-maker's wire

3 ready-made red tassels, 4 inches long

2 turban-style knots, each made from 2 yards of
⅛-inch-wide black cord

Leather flower petals, glued together to create
a flower

red & black tasseled wall decoration

This stunning wall decoration was inspired by African tribal headdresses and is made from a simple straw plate charger, which has been spray-painted black and then left to dry. A fringe made of turkey feathers was glued around the perimeter of the place mat, ¾ inch in from the edge. For a professional finish, black grosgrain ribbon was then glued around the edge to cover the heading tape and the seam. The tassel is the *pièce de résistance* (see steps below). To attach it, just push the wire through the center of the place mat and twist it at the back to secure.

1 Cut a piece of florist's wire 12 inches long and make a small loop at one end. Thread on one of the glass beads. Spread out the silky fringe and lay the wired bead on one end of the heading tape.

2 Wrap the end of the silky fringe around the bead and roll the enclosed bead along the heading tape, rolling up the fringe to create a tassel skirt. Then wind a piece of thin wire that is easy to bend—such as a narrow-gauge jewelry-maker's wire—around the neck of the tassel and twist to secure it.

3 Thread the three ready-made tassels onto a piece of wire and twist this around the neck of the silky tassel.

4 Thread one of the turban-style knots onto the central wire and glue it in place, pushing it down over the neck of the tassel to conceal the wires. Then thread on the leather flower, the second turban-style knot and the second glass bead.

braid baskets

Here is an excellent illustration of how to finish loose ends with a turban-style knot. I learned the simple technique of braiding at an early age, about the same time as tying shoelaces, and it's one I use over and over again. These great baskets are made of cord, but you could just as easily use strips of fabric for a softer look. Or, instead of making the cord braid into a basket, you could coil it flat to make a place mat, following the method on page 38—I love a technique to multitask. Baskets are such useful catch-alls, and a larger one could be used as a vegetable or bread basket. Alternatively, scale it down to make a pen holder.

1 Cut off 2 yards of cord and set it aside, then cut the remaining cord into three lengths of 6 feet each. Sew these three cords together at one end and braid them. Sew the other ends of the cord together to prevent the braid from unravelling. Working on a flat surface, coil the braided cord into a circle of approximately 8 inches in diameter.

2 Cut the piece of felt in a circle to fit the coiled cord and glue it onto the coil to keep it in place. This will become the base of the basket. Turn the coil over and start to build up the sides of the basket, placing the braided cord on top of the outer coil of the base. Sew the cord in place as you go, placing each successive coil directly on top of the previous one.

3 Make a turban-style knot out of the remaining 2 yards of cord (see pages 46–7) and glue it onto the end of the braided cord for a neat finish.

MATERIALS

20 yards of ½-inch-thick cord
Scissors
Needle and thread
Felt, 10 x 10 inches
Glue and glue gun

1

2

3

FROGGING

This is a decorative flat knot that can be fashioned in cord or ribbon. Traditionally used on military tunics or cuffs to signify rank, it can be used as an embellishment on everything from cushions to upholstery.

1 Loop the braided-string cord to the right and cross the long end over the short end. Continue into a figure-eight, making another loop at the bottom. Pass the end through the top loop and pull to make the loops smaller.

2 Continue, this time passing the long end over the bottom loop and under the short end.

3 Push the end in through the bottom loop and thread it under the short end. Thread it over the next cord and in through the last loop in the bottom-left corner. Pull the ends tightly.

4 For the "wagon wheels," cut two pieces of cord. Make a loop in the center of one to create a "buttonhole," crossing the cords and securing with a few stitches. Tie a double knot in the center of the other piece to form a "button." Coil the ends to form the "wheels" and glue.

5 Glue then stitch the "wheels" to the base of your frogging shapes to hide the raw ends.

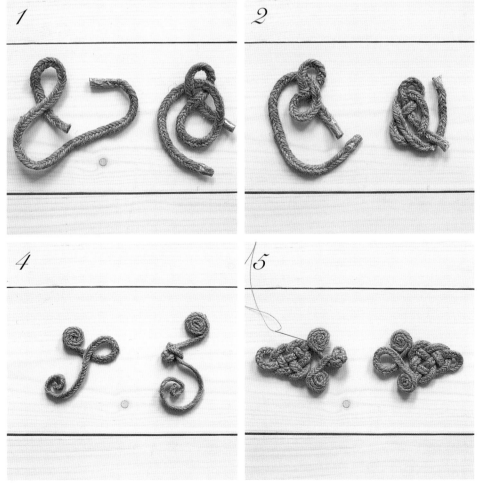

bullion doorstop

Slamming the door was a criminal offense when I was a child, and leaving the door open to let the bracing Cumbrian wind whistle through the house always resulted in an exasperated shout of "Shut the door!" This type of doorstop, made with wonderful bullion fringe, is a great way to prop doors open and prevent them from banging shut, however strong the draft or heavy the door. It is not the weight of the stop that prevents the door from slamming, its the fact that the long strands of the bullion fringe get stuck underneath the bottom of the door and jam it in place.

Bullion fringe is available in an endless array of colors, so you are sure to be able to find one that complements the décor of every room in the house. Some bullion fringes come with additional decorative fringe, braid, or tassels over the top of the basic fringe, and these would look superb in a grand room, especially in a large older home. Plainer designs in single colors will work best in a contemporary setting.

1 Turn the flower pot upside down. Using the glue gun, attach one end of the bullion fringe just above the rim of the pot, aligning the heading tape of the bullion with the rim of the flower pot, so the length of fringe trails onto the work surface below the rim.

2 Continue gluing the bullion fringe around the flower pot, turning the pot as you go and layering the rows of fringe up the sides until you reach the base of the pot, then glue the last row of bullion around the edge.

3 Cut 2½ yards of cord and, leaving 16 inches free at one end, make a turban-style knot (see pages 46–7). Thread the long end of cord through the hole in the base of the flower pot and pull the cord through to the inside so the turban-style knot sits centrally on top of the inverted pot. Thread the wooden bead onto the cord inside the flower pot, push the bead up to the top and secure with a knot to hold it in place.

4 To finish, glue the remaining 6 inches of cord around the base of the turban-style knot, filling in the gap between the top of the bullion fringe and the base of the decorative knot.

MATERIALS

Clay flower pot, 8 inches high with a 6-inch
   diameter base
Glue and glue gun
1 yard of bullion fringe, 6 inches deep
3 yards of ½-inch-thick cord
Scissors
Large wooden bead or piece of wood with
   a center hole

KNOTTING CORD

This is a very straightforward technique for knotting a single length of cord. It is very easy to master, quite addictive, and once you get the hang of it you will come up with all sorts of uses for it. Knotted cord is especially appropriate for easy curtain tiebacks (see opposite). Done on a smaller scale, with a ¼-inch-thick cord for example, it makes the perfect trim for covering nails and staples (see the edging used for the footstool on pages 82–3). Similarly, long lengths could encircle a chair seat, stool, or ottoman. As ever, think laterally, and up and down in terms of scale.

1 Make a slip knot at one end of a piece of cord. To do this, fold over the end, then make a loop next to it and pass the folded end through this loop from the back to the front.

2 Pull tight, so the short end is just visible at the base of the slip knot. Then make another loop next to the slip knot.

3 Pass this new loop through the first loop and pull tight, keeping the cord in a looped shape as you do so. Make another loop next to this second loop and repeat, passing this third loop through the second loop and pulling it tight.

4 Continue in this way until you have used up all the cord or until you have created enough knotted cord for its intended use, then pass the loose end through the last loop and pull tight to finish.

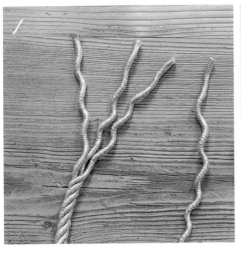

KNOTTED CURTAIN TIEBACK

This is an easy way to make professional-looking cord tiebacks that will dress up plain curtains beautifully. First make the "embrace"—the part of the tieback that will encircle the curtains—using the knotting technique shown opposite, then finish with trusty turban-style knots.

MATERIALS

5 yards of ½-inch-thick cord for a 32-inch tieback
4 feet of ½-inch-thick cord for each turban-style knot
16 inches of ½-inch-thick cord for the loops
Tape measure, scissors, and glue

1 Cut a piece of cord 16 inches long and split it in three. Use two strands to form a loop on each end of your knotted-cord tieback and discard the third.

2 Create the first loop by threading one of the strands though the last loop in your knotted cord. Form a circle and tie the ends together securely, then rotate the loop so the join is hidden.

3 Make a turban-style knot with 4 feet of cord (see pages 46–7). Pass the loop attached to the end of the knotted cord through the turban-style knot, making sure all ends are hidden inside the knot, then glue in place. Create another loop and knot at the other end of the cord in the same way. Encircle the curtain with the tieback and loop the ends over the hook on the window frame.

beads, shells & feathers

OPPOSITE Shells have been used as decorations for grottos, mirrors, boxes, and other seaside-themed ornaments for years and seem never to go out of fashion. A rare and precious natural resource, shells should always be bought from a reputable supplier or collected from local shores. THIS PAGE Chandelier crystals make wonderful decorations for a traditional wall light, as the intricate cuts and facets sparkle and catch the light in a magical way. Bugle-bead tassels and large crystal drops were hung from the fixture, attached with wire, while the wrapped-ribbon shades were embellished with simple glass beads sewn on at intervals. A hand-painted velvet flower and organdy ribbon add the finishing touches.

crystal drops to ostrich feathers

Glass is one of my favorite materials to work with, and I get endless ideas playing with crystal drops, beads, and wire. I love old chandeliers, not only as exquisite hangings when intact, but—better still—in pieces. Then I can use the components— rounds, squares, oblongs, almonds, or teardrops—for other decorative ideas, such as embellishing lights or creating glass curtains or wreaths (see pages 115 and 141).

My first experiment with the jewellike chandelier drops that I'd collected over the years was to hang them in lengths in a sunny window. The rainbow patterns this threw onto the walls, ceiling, and floor at certain times of the day were impressive and inspired me to attach individual drops to traditional braid for curtains, and finally to create trim for furniture such as sofas and chairs. You can simply hand-sew individual drops to ordinary upholstery trim and change the look instantly. When you don't have enough of the same shape, just mix and match for a true vintage feel.

Old glass has a crystal element and generally has more intricate cuts and facets than new glass, so it will sparkle more as the prisms catch and refract the light, giving a magical effect. New beads or semiprecious stones can be mixed in with old pieces to introduce color and other shapes. Artificial or "faux" glass, which is made from acrylic, gives the effect of vintage glass but is less sparkly than crystal. It is much lighter than

real glass, making it ideal for decorating smaller lampshades as well as for creating items such as flowers for napkin rings or centerpieces. It is available in colors such as pink, amber, gold, red, green, and amethyst.

I often wrap boring lamp stands with ribbon or cord, but I also find that threading glass beads onto lengths of wire and wrapping them around the lamp makes a stunning decorative base (see page 144). In addition, glass studs make wonderful alternatives to covered buttons on furniture with buttoned upholstery, especially when they are used with satin fabric— so chic and glamorous (see page 68). Studs can also be used to decorate chairs, padded headboards, or pillows (see page 102).

OPPOSITE An original and pretty way to decorate napkins is with shells glued to the ends of a piece of flexible wire and twisted together. The pearly sheen of the highly polished shells beautifully sets off the cream linen. I think this is one instance when we might have improved on nature, as shells do not have such a luster beneath the waves.
RIGHT Experimenting with wire, beads, and glass drops comes naturally to me, as I see the potential to create something for the home in objects of all shapes and sizes. This decorative lampshade is made from strands of wire with acrylic faceted beads in pale green and lilac attached at intervals, weighted at the bottom with long glass drops (see pages 154–5).

Shells have been used at least since Victorian times for all manner of decorative ideas, such as covering trinket boxes, mirrors, picture frames, tabletops, and even whole rooms with shells, as the many lovely examples of shell-encrusted grottos prove. Gluing shells all over the surface of such items is a great way to cover up a less-than-perfect finish and transform them into something really pretty. Delicate shell fringes can be hung over walls or windows, or draped around headboards and over mantelpieces. Wreaths or swags are easy to make and can be used in any room in the home, hung on a wall or over a doorway or fireplace (see pages 133–5). A decorative sculpture in its own right, a wreath could also be adapted to make a mirror or picture frame. Shells can look wonderful against a luxurious background, and I made a feature of a door by hanging a swag above it made of luscious chocolate-brown velvet with a wire-edged ribbon decorated with shells entwined through it (see page 116). Shells also look stunning piled up inside a glass bowl or vase and displayed as a centerpiece on a table. Another idea is to stand a plain table lamp in a large glass vase and fill it up with a variety of shells (see page 145). The Philippines is the main source of these exquisite treasures, but as shells are often from protected species, only certain types can be bought and sold. Always buy shells from a reputable licensed dealer who sells shells from a sustainable source.

Feathers are an embellishment of fantastic versatility and are surprisingly robust. You can sit on various sorts of ostrich plumes, for instance, without damaging them. They come in fringes and boas so can be attached in hundreds of ways. I love pale green ostrich as an edging on tablecloths, wall hangings, or throws. Most feather fringes are made from turkey plumes, dyed a rainbow of colors and cut to any size. I've used black turkey fringes 8 inches long on the base of a sofa. Use them on lampshades, sew them around a throw or along the leading edge of a curtain—imagine purple and black layered on peacock-green silk, with swags and tails for a fabulously decadent look. Make exquisite feather tassels or tie single feathers to a napkin—pheasant feathers, for example, will give a table setting an instant country look.

technique wiring beads

Any glass shape can be wired as long as it has a hole through which to attach it. Crystal is the best quality and gives the brightest sparkle, but artificial glass made from acrylic is lighter and available in a variety of contemporary decorative shapes and colors. Vintage chandelier glass mixed with colored beads give a unique and stylish look.

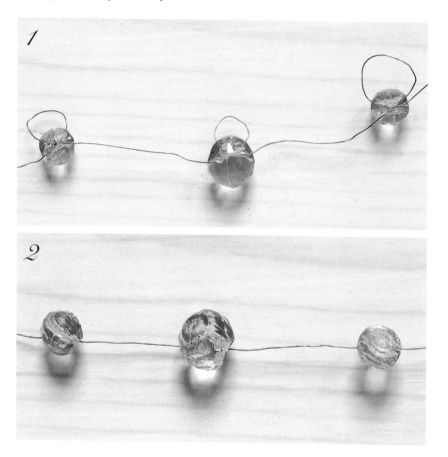

BEADS SPACED ON WIRE

Threading a series of beads onto a length of wire but keeping them a set distance apart from each other is not difficult. Here I have looped the wire around the beads to hold them in place, but a suitable glue could be used instead.

1 Thread on the first bead, passing the wire through the hole in the center. Hold the bead in position about 2 inches from the end of the wire, then pass the wire around the bead and back through the hole again, pulling the wire tight to make sure the bead stays in place.

2 With the first bead secured, thread on another bead. Hold it at the required distance in front of the first bead and pass the wire around the bead and back through the hole, pulling the wire tight as before. Repeat this method to add as many beads to the wire as you wish, spacing them at the required intervals.

BEADS WITH LARGE HOLES

When making a decorative hanging piece, it can be tricky to wire beads and other components that have large holes, but this technique will solve the problem every time.

1 When wiring a bead or other component that has a large hole, use a small bead to create a secure end. Working like a large knot, this "stopper" will keep the subsequent beads in place while also looking attractive. Thread a small bead onto the wire, pass it to the center point and fold the wire back on itself.

2 Twist the wires three times, just above the bead. Thread the double-thickness wire through the larger bead, now with the little "stopper" attached. Then thread on the other components.

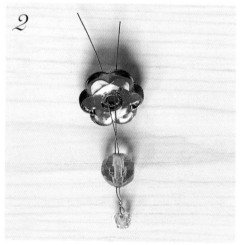

WIRE

In addition to being an indispensable tool, wire can be a great decorative medium in its own right—craftwork and jewelry wires come in many lovely colors as well as in various thicknesses. The thicker wire is galvanized and very easy to manipulate. Being so malleable makes it great for display work, as it twists perfectly on itself, securing objects in an instant and staying put. Never try to knot wire—it just doesn't work. Simply do the twist—three twists, in fact—and have faith—it won't come undone.

Some of the wires illustrated here are pretty enough to be left visible, so use them to secure the neck of a tassel. I have whole tassels made from wire, fashioned into bullion twists, netted tops, and elaborate flower shapes. In fact, eighteenth-century tassels are actually yarn-covered wire. Experiment with using colored wire overtly and also try concealing thinner wire inside tassel fringes. With the wide choice of wires available, you are sure to be able to find one that can be cunningly camouflaged or matched to whatever fringe, cord, or other trim you are working with.

One sort of florist's wire, known as "stub" wire, is a basic uncoated steel and is best suited to attaching displays of heavier fringes, foliage, or shells. Very much a utilitarian wire, it could even be used to make cabinet-door handles, finished with turban-style knots.

Often the type of wire you choose to use for a project will be determined by the size of the objects you are intending to wire. The larger they are, the more robust the wire needs to be. Make sure the wire will pass through the holes in any beads or components you wish thread on.

ABOVE This chair was old and battered with a gorgeous fabric falling off it in shreds, so I had a similar design reproduced, bringing out the colors in slightly more vibrant shades. The resulting English woven silk is a favorite fabric of mine. To glam up the skirt, I added a crystal fringe, which lies perfectly on the crease. You can create similar trims using old glass and crystal beads for the best sparkle. I won't lie—it's painstaking, but worth the effort.

OPPOSITE Two hanging flower baskets dangle upside down and metamorphose into an elegant chandelier. The shaped drops are glass not crystal, but they still give an opulent feel. Use any shapes you can lay your inventive hands on. I've added random lengths of crystal beads, and on a sunny day they bounce dancing prisms off the wall opposite.

technique wiring shells

When using shells for any kind of decoration, the problem is always how to attach them. The best way is with a hot glue gun (an investment you will never regret) and wire—the belt-and-braces no-risk approach. Remember, the heavier the shell, the more substantial the wire needs to be.

GLUING WIRE TO SHELLS

The idea is to make a tight coil at the end of a piece of wire, which gives a flat surface area to which the shell can be glued. The size of the coil will be determined by the size of your shell—the larger the shell, the bigger the coil will need to be to secure it. By the same token, the coil of wire must be small enough to fit inside the "inner ear" of the shell, so it's concealed on the inside where it won't be visible. There are usually ridges and undulations on the inside of the shell where the wire coil can find a foothold.

GLUE THE SHELL TO A COIL OF WIRE Take a length of florist's wire, long enough to wrap around or poke into whatever you intend to attach the shell to, and bend one end into a tight coil. Using a hot glue gun, squirt a large blob of glue into the inside or back of the shell. Push the coiled end of the wire into the glue and wait for it to dry.

WIRING SHELLS WITH HOLES

The easiest shells to use are those that have a small hole, so you can simply thread your wire through and twist to secure. Some shells have small natural holes, created before or after their original occupants moved out, but it is also possible to buy shells with a hole ready-drilled. This is a tricky process and needs to be done by a professional to prevent the shell from cracking or breaking.

THREAD THE SHELL ONTO WIRE Thread a length of wire through the hole in the shell. Fold the wire back on itself and twist the ends together three times to secure. The ends of the wire can then be used to attach the shell to your chosen object. In addition to wiring individual shells, you can follow this method to wire a cluster of shells together. Thread several shells onto the same piece of wire, one at a time, then fold the end of the wire back on itself and twist the two strands together as before.

THIS PAGE A seashell theme is ideal for summer dining in a sunroom, where the windows are draped with swags of delicate shell fringe. Antique coral decorates the table instead of flowers, and the centerpiece is a collection of beautiful shells of every shape and size, all placed on a runner of wide linen ribbon. Napkin rings are made from a length of wire with two shells for decoration, while the place cards are held within a cluster of shells that have been wired together and propped up on a coil of wire. Starfish decorate the chair backs.

technique feather trims

Feathers have long played a part in ceremonial events and displays in many cultures. Single plumes from nonprotected birds, such as turkey, pheasant, and chicken, are widely available and make very versatile trims. They can be dyed to wonderful colors and made into fringes that are surprisingly robust for valances, cushions, and lampshades.

SHAPING FEATHERS

This process helps shape feathers into whatever line or curve pleases you, such as the flowing curves of the long pheasant feathers used to trim the circular mirror on page 132.

STEAM THE FEATHER AND SHAPE To shape a feather, bring water to a boil in a tea kettle and, wearing oven gloves, hold the part of the feather that you wish to bend in the hot steam to soften it. When the feather is malleable, carefully bend it into shape and hold it in position until cool.

ATTACHING FEATHERS WITH WIRE

Wired feathers can be used for decorating items such as lampshades, curtains, and throws. To attach a feather to an item such as a lampshade, lay the feather in position and use a thick needle to pierce two holes ¼ inch apart on either side of the stem. Push one wire through each hole and twist the ends together on the reverse side to hold the feather in place.

WIRING FEATHERS Fold a length of thin silver wire around the end of the feather, with an equal amount of wire on each side. Twist the wires together with three turns to secure.

FEATHER FRINGE

There are plenty of ready-made feather fringes available in all sorts of plumages, depths, and colors, but it is also possible to make your own from scratch. This allows you to create a customized look, combining the plumage and colors of your choice within a single fringe.

1 Choose some inch-wide cotton tape for the heading in a color that either blends or contrasts well with your feathers. Lay the feathers side by side along the bottom half of the tape, aligning all the ends. Secure the feathers with a basting stitch.

2 Fold the top edge of the tape over the ends of the feathers and sew to enclose them securely within the heading.

1

2

THIS PAGE All shapes and sizes of lampshade are easy to cover with any fabric or trim—from ribbon and cord to feathered or bead fringe—it is all about manipulation of the material. Simply by wrapping and gluing, you can create wonderful lampshades covered in gold cord, silky fringe, raffia, or braid. Go to a fantastic trimmings shop and discover the wealth of trims you can use. This stunning feathered lampshade is wrapped in swathes of turkey-feather fringe, glued in place, and trimmed top and bottom with fluffy ostrich-feather fringe (see pages 148–9).

furniture

THIS PAGE I love to use unexpected items for certain jobs—and a particular favorite trick is to replace deep buttons with glass studs, which are just as easy to incorporate as buttons. Heavy satin for the upholstery enhances the chair's Hollywood-film-star glamour, with the glass studs glinting like flashbulbs on the red carpet. They are a delicate flower shape when you peer closely to admire them, with an exquisite sheen. In addition to studs and buttons for the dimples, add bead fringes to dress up the bottom edge.

OPPOSITE A chandelier-glass curtain made from individual strands of crystal drops creates a spectacular light show when sunlight hits the prisms and rainbow shadows are thrown across the whole room. A table lamp is decorated with crystal drops, and the shade is finished with long bead trim. The antique sofa is made yet more glamorous by the addition of real crystal drops on a trim around its base.

armchairs to ottomans

Reinventing a piece of furniture with ribbons and trims is exciting, whether it's a chair, sofa, table, or chest. When upholstering old pieces, people tend to play safe, but not me. If a favorite heirloom or secondhand find is looking tired and not quite trendy enough, the easiest way to give it a makeover is either to paint it or—far more versatile, colorful, and dramatic—to cover it with trims, ribbons, and fabric.

It is not difficult to wake up a piece of furniture and give it a stylish new look. If the base is essentially sound but the upholstery is looking past its best, cover it with a new fabric and edge it with a trim—ribbon, braid, beading, or cord—or, best of all, a combination of all four. I completely transformed a little chair by reupholstering it with a bold lemon-sherbet velvet that was used for millinery in the 1930s (see opposite). Small chairs such as this are ideal to work with—you don't need too much fabric, so they

provide a great opportunity to use up scraps of material or vintage remnants. The colors I choose are often inspired by nature—flowers, trees, fields, beaches, wherever the earth shows its magic. The yellow chair with its funky striped panel in shades of pink, mauve, and yellow reflects the gorgeous colors of the lilies in the vase next to it. Such a combination lifts my spirits.

I invariably start planning my design with a single ribbon or trim that catches my imagination. For instance, I gave an old chaise longue a new lease on life with a wonderful hand-dyed screen-printed fabric in deep purple and beige velvet (see page 102). My starting point for this design was a beautiful old jacquard ribbon, whose floral pattern had faded over the years to a subtle pale lilac and chocolate brown. I used this broad ribbon to trim the base, with a lilac velvet piping tape as an edging in the seams and fuchsia-pink velvet ribbon covering the deep-set buttons. This mix-and-match of velvet and satin is a key feature of my reinvention of antiques, which, like sculptural art installations, become centerpieces in contemporary spaces.

OPPOSITE When covering a piece of furniture with ribbon, choose a combination of ribbons and trims that will fit each panel exactly, or at least as closely as possible. For this chest of drawers (see pages 88–9), I used a marvelous grosgrain stripe, 3 inches and 2 inches wide, and a ¾-inch-wide woven wool braid interwoven with metallic yarn. Their widths fit the top of the chest and the drawers, and any gaps were filled with glass beads. RIGHT The fluorescent lemon-sherbet velvet used to upholster this little chair was used for millinery in the 1930s. The chair is trimmed with a gorgeous panel of candy-striped ribbons edged with bead fringe (see page 28). The lemon sherbet pulses against the pink, mauve, and yellow stripes—colors that seem to have been drawn straight from the lilies.

V V Rouleaux has an archive collection of ribbon design documents from the 1840s that have proved the springboard for many color schemes and designs; part of one of the ribbons inspired the fabric, called the "Chevron" design, used to upholster the sofa on page 12. Whichever ribbon I decide to use as my starting point, there is an incredible array of colors to work with—some so contemporary that you can hardly believe they date from the 1840s. One stunning example has a mauve background with a crisscross of stripes in black, beige, and red with a burgundy stripe running through it, edged with tartan plaid in beige, black, and taupe.

I am also very lucky to have a collection of wonderful vintage ribbons, and I love to use these precious lengths to turn an otherwise plain piece of furniture into an eye-catching focal point. The yellow campaign chair on page 76 has been promoted to a key player with its wide central striped band.

There are endless possibilities for applying ribbon or braid to furniture, and you can cover most surfaces, even if they are curved or irregular. Ribbons can be sewn, glued, or stapled in place, depending on the surface you are attaching them to. You can either cover a surface completely with ribbon, butting each one up to the next and smoothing them flat (such as on the chest of drawers, left and pages 88–9), or just use them as edging or trimming (see, for example, the chairs on pages 72–3 and 78–9). Ribbons can be joined together widthwise (as on the chair, right, and the bench, pages 96–7), or woven together and applied as a panel (see the table on pages 80–1 and the ottomans on pages 86–7). Adding fringes to an existing chair cover is easy, as they can be stitched straight onto the fabric; similarly, braid can be sewn around the edges of cushions to give a sofa a fresh look. Attaching tassels is another stylish way to embellish the arms of couches or armchairs, or dress up the backs of dining chairs—go for a vibrant mauve glass extravagance as seen on page 74. If you can't find enough beads and bits, try thrift shops and yard sales for old necklaces to break up, and round glass components for incorporating into tassels. Scraps of fabric can also be recycled with imagination. Don't limit yourself to upholstery braids; use fashion trims, too.

chairs, sofas, & tables

I love unusual, quirky pieces of furniture that have lots of character and potential, so I'm always drawn to old-fashioned shapes—and mostly to chairs with deep-buttoned upholstery. Doing up furniture gives you the opportunity to play with color and experiment with different looks to create truly unique pieces. Don't always choose safe color combinations; try clashing bold hues and patterns as well. For instance, I might use a tartan-plaid edging next to a floral design, followed by a stripe. I also like to mix several different textures together—velvet fabric, striped grosgrain ribbons, and bright pink glass beads, for example. Before you commit yourself, pin your chosen trims onto the piece in question and see how it looks in situ. Some of the most amazing ribbon designs date from the early nineteenth century. The color combinations are so contemporary that I often use them as a starting point for the design of a chair. In fact, you can create a whole room around these color schemes, starting with just a ribbon and building up from there.

ABOVE The ribbon used to trim this pale blue satin chair has a velvet stripe on one edge and a picot design on the other, with a satin gingham center— a great mixture of textures. The ribbon has been pleated over the curved arms and back of the chair and sewn in place. Glass flower studs, used instead of buttons, make the chair back more glamorous. The shell wreath carries through my favorite color combination of pale blue, brown, and beige, while the shell-filled lamp base continues the theme (see pages 133–5 and 145).
OPPOSITE On the back of the same chair is a central panel formed by a lovely 8-inch-wide vintage ribbon, which has a wonderful mixture of textures—satin and velvet with a fur edge. Whichever way it is positioned, this little chair is always a talking point.

OPPOSITE This dining chair is a great shape and makes a va-va-voom statement for a soirée, like a lady with an hourglass figure in a knock-'em-dead dress. A sensational tassel of semiprecious amethyst chips, topped off with a velvet flower head, hangs down the low-cut back. The edge of the seat has a jacquard picot-edge ribbon sewn around it. For the kitchen, you could do a girl-next-door version with wooden beads and a fresh flower from the garden—like Rita Hayworth and Doris Day, both beauties, but with different styles.

RIGHT Dressing tables are a must for girls. My own is large and, as may be imagined, covered with fabric flowers, ribbons collected over the years, and my most sentimental bits and pieces, with jewelry strewn about and hanging off every corner. This one is pretty and delicate and its metal curlicues are ideal for suspending stray hair accessories, bags, and ribbons. The stool, which has hand-embroidered birds on the top, is an old design that I had copied and called my "Wrap Stool." To match the curtains in this bedroom, I delicately stitched the floaty organdy ribbons to the edge and cinched in the "waist" with two other lengths of organdy streamers.

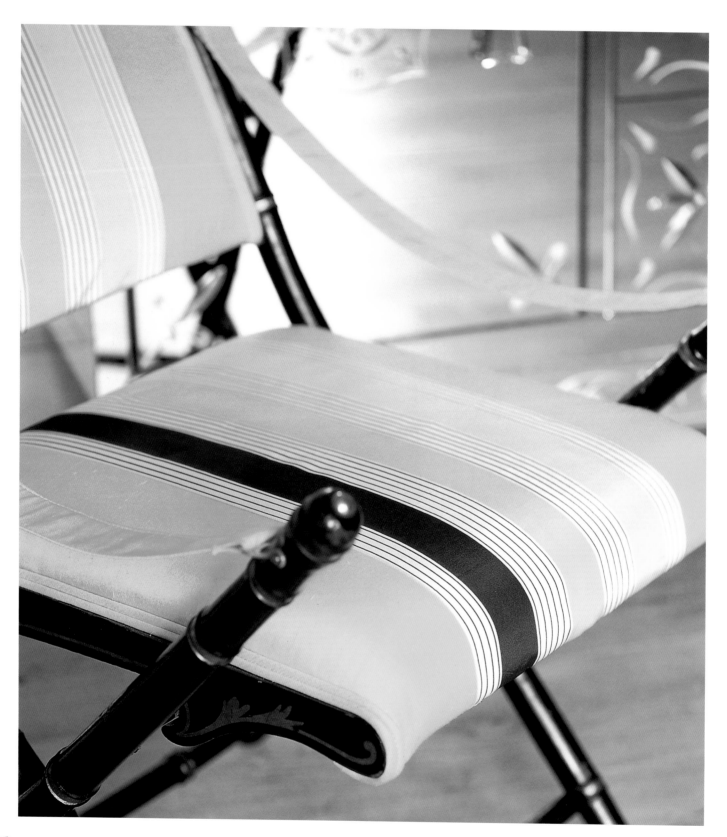

OPPOSITE I am very lucky to have a collection of vintage extra-wide ribbons. The one used here is a marvelous stripe of faded blue, black, and shades of yellow. The egg-yolk yellow of the chair matches perfectly. The ribbon has been stretched tight around the center of the chair seat and back and glued on the underside with the raw edge folded under for a neat finish. If you can't find a ribbon wide enough, this look can be achieved with several ribbons attached separately or fused together with iron-on interfacing (see page 28).

THIS PAGE The combination of colors in this gorgeous wide ribbon is so modern that you would never guess it is a Victorian design. The ribbon has been glued around the base of a cream upholstered sofa, and a stunning rosette and tassel in harmonizing colors have been sewn onto the end of each arm. The rosette is made from a piece of ribbon gathered tight along one edge to form a circle (see page 22); for instructions for a similar tassel, see pages 48–9. This is another case of a fabulous ribbon suggesting how to transform a dejected piece of furniture.

revamped red chair

To design your new-look chair, choose good quality cord, ribbon, and trim in a mix of textures and in colors and designs that will make a real impact. I used cord with a very vibrant bright pink to bring out the red in the chair fabric and the crimson in the vintage ribbon. The ribbon itself incorporates black velvet, magenta-and-gray checks, and lovely magenta picot edges—who would have thought to put that stunning combination together? Before you begin, pin all your chosen trims onto the chair to check that you're happy with the design and color combination.

MATERIALS

Button-backed chair
Tape measure
String
Scissors
3 yards of ½-thick cord
Glue and glue gun
2¼ yards bead trim, 2 inches deep
Pins
Needle and thread
3½ yards of 3-inch-wide vintage ribbon
1¼ yards of ⅝-inch-wide wire-edged ribbon

1 To figure out how much of each trim you will need to revamp your chair, it can be helpful to use a length of string to follow all the contours that you wish to cover with each type of cord or ribbon. Take these measurements and add an extra inch to each. Cut the cord to the correct length and begin gluing it onto the chair, starting at the bottom edge on one side and working your way up the side of the chair, over the back and down the other side, finishing on the bottom edge where the end will be overlapped by the ribbon. Use any trim that is already on the chair as your guide, either removing it and replacing it with new cord, or butting the new cord up against the existing trim, as here.

2 Pin the bead trim along the bottom edge of the chair, positioning it so the heading tape will be covered by the ribbon. Then sew it in place.

3 Pin the vintage ribbon along the bottom edge of the chair, covering the ends of the cord and the heading of the bead trim. Neatly sew in place.

4 Cut the wire-edged ribbon into 3-inch lengths and make each piece into a small rosebud (see page 22). You will need one rosebud to decorate each button on the button-backed chair. Sew a ribbon rosebud over each button.

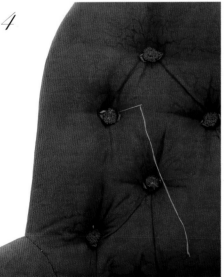

woven stool with long fringe

This old dressing-table stool needed updating, so I chose to do a woven-ribbon top with a fun fringe in wool and pleated ribbon. The neutral cream and chocolate-brown colors will blend with any interior scheme. The double-layered long wool fringe hides the stool's rather ugly legs. If you can't find a suitable fringe, you could always knot lengths of yarn together and sew them to the edges of the ribbon.

MATERIALS

16½ yards each of 1-inch-wide grosgrain ribbon in chocolate brown and cream
Scissors
Soft board and pins
28 x 28 inches square of heavy-duty iron-on interfacing and iron
28 inches of 2¾-inch-wide wool-and-linen mix chocolate-brown pleated ribbon
1½ yards of cream wool fringe, 12 inches deep
Needle and thread
Stool, approximately 20 inches in diameter
Staple gun

1 Cut the brown and cream ribbons into lengths of 24 inches. With right sides facing down, pin the brown ribbons side by side along one edge of the soft board and fold back alternate ribbons. Working in the other direction and with the right side facing down, lay a cream ribbon over the brown ribbons, and pin at each end. Fold down the brown ribbons, then lift up the adjacent brown ribbons. Continue weaving the ribbons in this way, following the technique on pages 29–30.

2 Lay the iron-on interfacing on top of the woven ribbons and iron to fuse the fabrics, following the manufacturer's instructions; remove the pins.

3 Cut the wool fringe into two lengths and pin one along both edges of the pleated ribbon, then sew.

4 Cut the woven ribbon to fit the top of the stool, allowing an extra inch all around to fold down over the edge. Using a staple gun, staple the ribbon fabric around the edge of the stool.

5 Pin the pleated ribbon around the edge of the stool, over the staples. Fold back the top row of fringe and staple the ribbon to the stool, top and bottom, directly under the top row of fringe—when you fold this back down, it will hide the staples.

1

layered ribbon footstool

There is nothing better than resting your feet on a footstool when you are relaxing and doing a bit of reading—your legs are elevated to just the right height. This old footstool was originally covered with a lovely but worn fabric, so I reinvented it for a more colorful contemporary feel. For this layering technique I have used 1½-inch-wide grosgrain ribbons in a rainbow of rich colors that all work well together—plum, rust, orange, gold, fuchsia, and mauve.

MATERIALS

Footstool, 14 inches in diameter

16 inches of 2oz batting, cut to size

Scissors

Pins

Staple gun

14 pieces, each 14 inches long, of 1½-inch-wide grosgrain ribbon in a variety of colors

3¼ yards of ⅛-inch-thick plum cord made into ⅜-inch-wide knotted trim (see page 54)

Glue and glue gun

24 inches of ⅛-inch-thick orange cord

5 pieces, each 2 inches long, of ½-inch-wide grosgrain ribbon in a variety of colors

Small glass flower stud

1 Remove the old fabric from the footstool. Trim the batting into a circular shape to fit over the top of the footstool and pin it in place; attach securely using a staple gun, removing the pins as you go. Cut pieces of ribbon long enough to fit centrally across the footstool from one edge to the other. Staple each ribbon at one side, then the other, ⅜ inch in from the bottom edge of the stool. Continue until the stool is covered with strips of ribbon, overlapping each piece as you go.

2 Make a knotted trim with the plum cord (see page 54) and glue it around the stool to hide the staples.

3 Glue the orange cord below the knotted trim.

4 For the ribbon rosette, make a fishtail cut on both ends of the ½-inch-wide ribbon pieces (see page 20). Pierce a hole through the center of each with the glass stud. Glue to the middle of the stool.

2

3

4

ruched wired table

I found this three-legged table in a French flea market and was attracted by its clover-leaf shape. The top was worn and I was excited to think of a new look for it, inspired by the type of French cupboards that have doors made of wire netting backed with fabric—usually faded gingham or tulle. I covered the tabletop with large roses made from 2¾-inch-wide wire-edged ribbon in mushroom beige shot with delicate blue, which I could manipulate to fit its shape. These were held in place with chicken wire and the table edged with ruched wired-edged taupe ribbon.

MATERIALS

13½ yards of 2¾ inch-wide wire-edged shot taffeta ribbon, plus extra for filling in (see step 3)
Needle and thread
Table, approximately 18 inches in diameter
3 yards of 4-inch-wide chicken wire
Wire cutters
8 feet of 25-gauge craft wire
Staple gun
6½ yards of 1-inch-wide wire-edged ribbon
Glue and glue gun

1 Cut the 2¾-inch-wide ribbon into 3 lengths of 4½ yards and pull the wires to ruche (see page 21).

2 Fold over one end of each ruched ribbon to form a central bud, then coil the rest into a large rose shape and sew the base to hold (see page 22).

3 Arrange the roses on the tabletop so they cover the surface. If necessary, fill in any space between the roses with ruched ribbon.

4 Cut the chicken wire into 6 lengths of 18 inches. Lay the strips side by side and bind them together using 18-inch-lengths of craft wire threaded through.

5 Place the wire on top of the roses and fold it tightly over the edges of the tabletop. Staple the wire all around the edge, then trim off the excess.

6 Ruche the 1-inch-wide ribbon and glue it all around the edge of the tabletop, concealing the cut edges of the wire and the staples.

OPPOSITE I think that combining different textures creates the most interesting interior. Here a taffeta throw has been trimmed with an ostrich-feather fringe. A satin woven pillow is edged with glass beads, and the top of the ottoman is covered with woven organdy ribbons, which also features a very thin rayon ribbon traditionally used for the hanging loops on garments. This has a great sheen to it and is a very underestimated ribbon. The lampshade is wrapped in wire-edged taffeta ribbon in deep purple, with two porcelain flowers wired on one side.

RIGHT This box was originally used for storing toys, but when the children had grown up and the once-fought-over contents had been passed on, I reclaimed it for books and the children's journals. The lid is covered with a woven design of mixed velvet and dotted ribbon, framed with looped red chenille. The box shape is perfect for displaying a variety of fringes. Behind is a vintage comforter embellished with stitched grosgrain ribbon and a multitude of crochet motifs.

storage Plenty of flexible storage is essential in a home, especially when you have four children and not enough closet space. There is no reason at all for it not to be stylish. The lovely name for an end-of-bed chest, ottoman, we may deduce derives from the great Ottoman Empire, which survived from the late thirteenth century to the early twentieth. The omnipotent sultan had a council of viziers known as a divan (maybe they lolled about a lot and thus named another piece of bedroom furniture), and perhaps he needed a big box in which to keep their heads if he didn't like their tone. Maybe the sultan sent one to England's Henry VIII? Who knows, but either way I think they deserve to be opulently covered. The pea-green one opposite is topped with the finest weave of ribbon—delicate organdy, rayon tapes, and small chenille yarns. It stores our winter clothes or sometimes bats, tennis rackets, and hockey sticks.

ribbon-covered chest with knot handles

My son was so fed up that his room was used for sewing and watching TV while he was away at school that I thought up this way to transform his shabby old chest of drawers to make it up to him. I covered it with a grosgrain ribbon of my own design, which won the House and Garden award for best trimming in 2003. The colors were inspired by my ribbon design documents from 1840—contrasting blues for boys, of course. This striped ribbon comes in endless widths, and I used a combination of 2-inch and 3-inch to make it easier to fill in the drawer fronts and the top and side panels, which are all different sizes. In addition, I used a ½-inch-wide woven wool braid interwoven with a metallic yarn and a glass bead trim to finish the top edge. I attached the ribbons to the chest using a hot glue gun, but other glues are fine, too. Take care not to use too much, though, as this will cause bumps under the ribbon.

You can cover most surfaces with ribbon or braid, even curved ones. Always butt up or meet adjacent ribbons, disguise any gaps with a trim and finish the edges with narrow braid to cover up the cut ends of the ribbons. If you have to attach handles, try to make the ribbons meet on each side; if this isn't possible, make a hole in the ribbon and finish with PVA glue to prevent it from fraying.

While I was in the mood for revamping, I wrapped an old picture frame in layer upon layer of waxed cord and made these great turban-style knot handles (see below).

MATERIALS

For each handle:

1 yard of ⅛-inch-thick waxed cord

1 yard of ¼-inch-thick waxed cord

Horn bead, 3 inches long

Glue and glue gun

1 Following the technique described on pages 46–7, make one large turban-style knot 1⅜ inches in diameter using 1 yard of ¼-inch-thick waxed cord. Next, make two smaller turban-style knots ½ inch in diameter using 14 inches of ⅛-inch-thick cord for each one. Push the large turban-style knot onto the center of the long horn bead.

2 Glue the smaller turban-style knots onto the ends of the long horn bead. Then cut 8 inches of ⅛-inch-thick cord and push one end through the first turban-style knot, through the center of the bead and out through the second turban-style knot. When the handle is finished, pass the ends of the waxed cord through the holes in the drawer front and knot together securely on the inside.

ribbon-covered bedside table

My daughter loved this table the way it was, but plain brown pieces are not part of my plan. A combination of vintage velvet, striped grosgrain, and wool braids turned the little brown hen into a peacock, which was received back with great enthusiasm. I used the wool braid as my color chart and selected the other elements to go with it. If the ribbon you are using is not very thick or doesn't have a rough texture, glue may show through. I used double-sided tape for this project, which also means the covering is easy to rip off when you feel like a change.

MATERIALS

Bedside table, body measuring
    approx. 12 x 14 x 10 inches
20 inches of red velvet fabric
Scissors
Double-sided tape
1 yard of ⅝-inch-wide stitched
    yellow grosgrain ribbon
24 inches of 1-inch-wide brown
    grosgrain ribbon
12 inches of 1-inch-wide red
    velvet ribbon
3½ yards of 12-inch-wide
    knitted wool braid
1 yard of 2-inch-wide striped
    grosgrain ribbon
12 inches of ⅝-inch-wide
    yellow ribbon

1 Cut a piece of velvet to fit the tabletop, adding an extra ¼ inch all around to overlap the edge. Cut three pieces of velvet to fit the back and side panels of the table. Apply double-sided tape around the edges of each panel, remove the backing and stick the velvet panels in place.

2 Using double-sided tape, attach the stitched grosgrain ribbon around the top edge of the tabletop, hiding the folded-down velvet.

3 Attach the brown grosgrain and red velvet ribbon to the frame above and below the drawers. Then cover the legs with ribbon. I used a mixture of knitted wood braid and striped grosgrain ribbon.

4 Cover the drawers with the striped grosgrain and yellow ribbon, cutting a slot for the handles.

laundry basket

Having a laundry basket in your bathroom or bedroom stops everyone from throwing their dirty clothes on the floor—I am a great one for keeping messy things out of sight. The pretty blue cord and pompoms are fun, and make the basket a decorative feature. I love the three shades of blue together, as well as the combination of the fluffy pompoms with the sleek twisted cord. It is easy to follow the contours of most regular-shaped objects, which suggests to me that they should all be covered with trims. The handle for the lid is easily pushed through the coir and is held in place with a simple knot. I have two baskets trimmed in different colors—one for washing and one for ironing.

1 Glue one end of cord along the bottom edge of the basket and continue to wrap it around, working your way up the sides. As you layer the cord around the basket, butt each coil closely to the one below, securing the cord with glue at regular intervals. When you have covered the bottom third of the basket, cut the cord at one of the back corners, wrapping the area you intend to cut through with clear tape to prevent the cut ends from fraying (see page 37).

2 Start the pompom tape at the corner where the cord ends and continue wrapping the basket. When you have used up the pompom tape, cover the rest of the basket with more of the cord.

3 Cut a piece of cord 18 inches long and push each end from front to back through the center of the lid, making sure the ends go through directly opposite each other and about 6 inches apart. Knot each end of the cord on the underside of the

lid. Then start to cover the top of the lid with cord, leaving space along the very bottom edge of the rim for the wooden-bead fringe.

4 Follow the contours and shape of the lid, gluing the cord in place as you go, especially where you make a turn at the corners. Finally, glue the wooden-bead fringe around the bottom edge of the lid to finish.

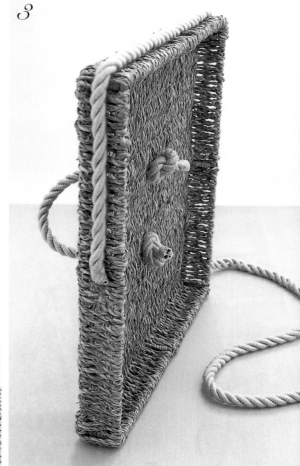

For a laundry basket measuring
   24 x 12 x 12 inches:
38 yards of ½-inch-thick cord
Glue and glue gun
Clear tape
Scissors
22 yards of pompom tape, 1¼-inch
   diameter pompoms
1½ yards of wooden-bead fringe,
   3 inches deep

outdoors While children are more than happy sprawling on a blanket on the ground, grown-ups tend to prefer sitting in a chair for a picnic—whether it is in the backyard, at the park, or on the beach. Any chairs with canvas slings, especially deckchairs, soon get brittle after being left out in the sun—or rain—over the summer. You sit down gingerly, waiting for the moment when the canvas splits and you find yourself wedged between chair and turf. So, reinforce the canvas by sewing a lovely strong linen ribbon or two on top. Bright colors stand out, so you can easily find your picnic spot when you return from a walk or swim. I went to the seaside only twice as a child and I loved the striped windbreaks pushed into the sand. I made one on a wooden base with tent pegs attached to anchor it, so you can put it on grass or sand. It works in light winds, but I wouldn't take your chances in a gale force. Its ribbons are a flag-waving world of multicolored stripes.

ABOVE If you wish to replace old deckchair canvas, make a good note of how it was attached. Alternatively, reinforce or rejuvenate canvas by stitching on ribbons. A heavy braid, webbing tape, or tightly woven ribbon are most suitable—don't use flimsy organdy for this job.

RIGHT Cords found in hardware stores are utilitarian rather than decorative, to be put to use on construction sites and boats. Their hard-wearing quality makes them ideal for wrapping outside furniture.

OPPOSITE A colorful outdoor scene has been created with a wonderful array of ribbons. The plain picnic blanket has been turned into a party rug with gingham tufts sewn around the edge (see page 40). The portable screen has a wooden base drilled with holes to hold bamboo poles. Lengths of ribbon were glued to the end pole and then woven across, behind and in front of alternate poles. The folding stools are a great design and lightweight enough to move easily. I replaced the old canvas seats with new ones made of woven ribbon backed with canvas and stapled onto the frame (see pages 29–30).

outside-inside bench

When I needed extra seating for a dinner party, I upholstered the slats of a garden bench to make it more comfortable and suitable for use indoors. It was an effective solution, but only possible if the bench has detachable slats. Once the bench has been reassembled, the bolts that secure the slats will conceal the hole made in the ribbon to enable the bolts to pass through (see step 3). Textured grosgrain ribbon is ideal, as it is hard-wearing and easy to work with, and available in a variety of widths, designs, and colors. The plain ribbon used for the backs of the slats creates an interesting contrast with the striped fronts.

MATERIALS

3 yards of 2oz batting

Scissors

3 yards of muslin

Tape measure

Hammer and tacks

Strong, textured ribbon such as 4-inch-wide
 striped grosgrain

2¾-inch-wide grosgrain ribbon for the back of the
 slats in a contrasting or harmonizing color

Pins

Sewing machine and thread

Glue and glue gun

1 Remove the slats from the bench and number them. For each slat in turn, cut the batting 1½ inches longer than each slat and wide enough to wrap around it with the edges overlapping. Cut the muslin to the same length and 1½ inches wider. Lay the batting on top of the muslin and place the slat on top. Fold one edge to the center and tack. Fold the other edge to the center, turning the muslin under for a neat finish, and tack along the length of the slat. Fold in the ends and tack.

2 Measure the covered slat to check how wide the ribbon needs to be to fit around it. You will need to sew together several lengths of ribbon to get the correct fit. I joined two lengths of 4-inch-wide striped ribbon and one length of 2¾-inch-wide red ribbon to create a single piece. Cut the ribbons 1½ inches longer than the slat. Pin, then sew them together using a sewing machine.

3 With right sides together, fold the ribbon fabric in half and pin, then sew, the outer edges together to create a long tube. Turn the tube right-side out and slide it over the covered slat, with the plain ribbon at the back of the slat. Ease the fabric gently until it lies smooth with an equal amount of loose fabric at both ends. Fold the ends under neatly and secure them with glue. Finally, use scissors to pierce a small hole in the ribbon to let the bolts that fasten the slats pass through. Repeat for each slat and then reassemble the bench.

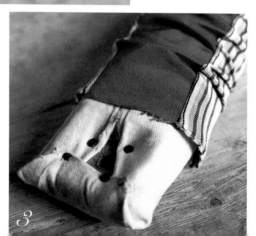

pillows & bed linen

scatter cushions to comforters

Embellishing pillows, cushions, and bed linen with ribbons and other decorative trimmings offers endless design possibilities. Ribbon and braid can be used simply as edging, or it may be woven, pleated, layered, ruched, frayed, or made into flowers, rosettes, or tufts. Small-scale items such as scatter cushions also provide a great opportunity to experiment with new looks and combinations of colors and textures.

PREVIOUS PAGE, LEFT
There's no point in collecting buttons only to keep them hidden in a button box. I used some of my favorites to decorate this pillow so I could admire them every day.
PREVIOUS PAGE, RIGHT
You can show off your entire collection of trims on a woven pillow covers, with ribbons, cords, and tassel and bead fringes incorporated into the weave (see pages 29–30).

When it comes to cushions and decorative pillows, you can make covers from scratch—for example, by weaving ribbons and fusing them together with iron-on interfacing to create a fabric (as on pages 99 and 105)—or simply decorate an existing pillow with anything from ribbons, braids, and fringes to buttons, feathers, and brooches (see pages 98 and 108–9). Different textures can be combined to great effect. One easy technique is to sew one ribbon with another in a random running stitch—for example, a 2-inch-wide plum grosgrain looks fantastic stitched with a fine pale blue ombré ribbon (see page 24). These stitched ribbons can then be sewn onto a pillow cover in horizontal rows, with stitches securing each end and one line of stitches running vertically through the center. This method of attaching the ribbons retains the loose edges and prevents the individual ribbons from looking like a single piece of pleated fabric. Using a mix of colors and different widths and textures within a weave—as with the pillow on page 99, which features cords, woven ribbons, beaded wire, tassels, and bead fringes—is a great way to show off a collection of ribbons and trims and a thrifty way to use up scraps. Layer fabrics, with the heaviest at the bottom and the sheerest on top, and incorporate delicate trims and ribbons. Fine nets are ideal for overlaying, allowing you a glimpse of the vintage treasure beneath (see pages 108–9). Millinery velvet has a beautiful sheen and makes the sort of pillows you would recline against at Le Moulin Rouge (see page 102).

I never pass a secondhand store without going in, and these forays often yield exquisite vintage bed linen and comforters in beautiful prints. Snap them up when you see them, as they make great toppers for beds. Customize them with trims and pompom braids in apple green, berry reds, and rosehip pink. They will look like new and cost a fraction of the price they sell for in retro-hip boutiques. When it comes to

OPPOSITE The faded vintage comforter is embellished with trims in shades of fruit found in a country hedgerow. If you don't have a weekend bolt-hole, bring a little "rus in urbis" to your inner-city bed.

RIGHT Outside entertaining gives you free rain when choosing colors, and these layered cloths of different sizes would be effective in any combination. The top cloth has been edged with 4-inch-deep orange bead fringe, while a clear bead fringe with emerald ends has been sewn on the second cloth. The fringes weigh the cloths down and prevent them from blowing away. The napkins in the braided raffia baskets (see page 50) are wrapped with thin cord in mixed primary colors tied in simple bows.

reinvention, heavy linen sheets, like the ones used in French hospitals or British prisons in the 1930s and 1940s, have great versatility. They are easy to dye and sew on, so they make a good base for embellishing. They are also useful for upholstery, as they wear very well. Plain bed linen provides a blank canvas for decorative trimming, but make sure you use a ribbon or braid that is washable and hard-wearing. You could even fashion a family or personal monogram out of ribbon—if you are snazzy enough. Whatever you decide, remember to put your decorative trim on the inside top edge of the sheet, so it is showing on the outside when you turn down the corner at night. My ambition is to have a dedicated linen closet or even a walk-in laundry room with rows of shelves heaped with perfectly pressed folded linen sheets, pillowcases and towels—all bearing my monogram. I have four beautiful buttermilk-colored sheets with a monogram on the fold-down edge, which I carefully iron when wet to present them completely flat and crisp. At the beginning of the nineteenth century, some city dwellers would send their linen to be washed and dried in the clean country air. It would return ironed and sealed, and when unfurled it would smell fresh as a daisy, literally. These days we don't have a "wash day," and very few people hang their sheets outside to dry, but when I was little, the sheets would be picked up by the laundry van on a Thursday and returned the following Monday wrapped in fantastic paper of pale blue, pink, lilac, and white stripes, tied with pale blue cotton tape. My memory of this paper is what inspired the ribbon used to edge the rug on page 138.

Another great use for odds and ends of ribbons and trimmings is to cover your coat hangers (see pages 112–13). When you open your closet doors to choose the day's outfit, you are greeted by a glorious array of cheerful colors. How extravagant it would be to have winter hangers and summer hangers—leather, suede, velvet, faux fur, tweed, and animal print in rich colors for winter, and organdy, satin, silk, metallic braid, bead fringe, and pretty floral prints in pinks, blues, and lilacs for summer. Alternatively, make your scraps into rosettes (see page 23) and award them to a pillow.

pillows When scatter cushions become tired and lose their vibrancy, this is the time to trim them to death. Hundreds of ideas come to mind, from adding tassels or bead fringes to layering ribbons and trims. Make a new stripe concoction, for instance, with turquoise, purple, orange, red, green, and pink grosgrain (see technique on page 28), and add tassel fringes and bead trims on top. Sew this on a cushion and glue wool braid over the edges. Old pillows from thrift shops are often filled with soft goose down which are the best to embellish. Attach a really wide ribbon down the center, stitched at each end (see page 110), or sew layers of deep silky fringe across the cover, similar to the bullion pillow on page 104. Try out all these ideas, then pile your beribboned, buttoned, and trimmed pillows on the sofa.

LEFT Although traditionally used to edge the base of sofas, this deep bullion fringe makes an unusual and stylish pillow cover and demonstrates that you are limited only by your imagination as to what type of trims can be applied where. This contemporary "dreadlocked" pillow is simply layers of black bullion fringe sewn one above the other. It comes in a wide choice of colors to suit any scheme.

OPPOSITE Weaving ribbon is a very versatile technique—whether woven on a stiff backing of self-adhesive plastic, woven and backed with iron-on interfacing, or simply stitched at all the crossover points (see pages 29–30). These fine pillows are made from narrow satin ribbons woven and secured with iron-on interfacing—a real labor of love to create. I like to use really prominent trims that make a statement, so I added large pear-shaped beads in purple and pink.

BELOW Perfect for a feminine bedroom, these small organdy pillows have embroidered silk flowers and pleated ruched edges.

PREVIOUS PAGE, LEFT These sumptuous pillows are made from millinery velvet dating from 1930–40. The vibrant colors and sheen of the fabric are enhanced by the flower-shaped glass studs, which are arranged in different designs on each pillow.

PREVIOUS PAGE, RIGHT The pale blue velvet pillow has been overlaid with a panel of white millinery net to add texture. The cover is bordered with mother-of-pearl buttons, and the net panel is scattered with vintage patterned or covered buttons.

ruched frayed-edge pillow

This gorgeous silk pillow is rich in texture and subtle shades of purple and lilac. The edge, which joins the top and bottom pieces of the cover, is made from a ruched wire-edged taffeta ribbon with plum-colored frayed inserts; a mauve feather rosette is the finishing touch. The chair is upholstered in shot-silk "Iris" fabric, woven in Britain, and this inspired the colors used for the pillow. They work well with the color scheme of the room and ribbon paneling on the walls.

1 Cut the 2-inch-wide ribbon in half. Cut the wire off one edge and fray (see page 20), then pull the wire on the other edge and gather (see page 21). Repeat to create two ruched frayed fringes.

2 Cut out two circles from the silk fabric, 12 inches in diameter. Pin one fringe around the edge of each circle, with the gathered edge pinned to the right side of the silk, then stitch.

3 Evenly ruche the 2¾-inch-wide ribbon by pulling on the wires at both edges.

4 With right sides facing out, pin, then sew the ruched ribbon around the edge of one of the circles, covering the seam where you have joined the frayed ribbon to the silk. Then pin the bottom piece of the pillow cover to the other edge of the ruched ribbon and sew to halfway.

5 Insert the pillow form and finish by hand.

6 To make a feather rosette, roll up the edge of the feather fringe, stitching the ends together as you go. Fan out the feathers and stitch the base to the center of the pillow.

MATERIALS

4½ yards of 2-inch-wide wire-edged ribbon

Scissors

16 inches silk fabric

Pins, needle, and thread

Sewing machine

2 yards of 2¾-wide wire-edged ribbon

Pillow form, 12-inch diameter

1 yard of feather fringe, 3¼ inches deep

layered pillow

I talk a lot about my bits-and-pieces box, stuffed full of ribbons, trims, decorative motifs, and bits of old jewelry. This pillow is a lovely way to display some small heirloom pieces, such as a broken brooch or pendant from a necklace, which can be sewn on. The design can incorporate anything from feathers and beads to small pieces of braid and ribbon. The pillow itself is not old, but once you have attached the decorations and covered them with the veil, it could be a vintage piece.

MATERIALS

41 inches of 6-inch-wide fur-
    trimmed vintage ribbon
41 inches of bead trim,
    1 inch deep
Scissors
Pins
Needle and thread
Tape measure
Pillow, 20 x 28 inches
Selection of feathers, brooches,
    or other decorative trimmings
20 x 12 inches veiling or net

1 Cut the ribbon and bead trim in half. Pin, then sew one piece of trim along the outer edge of each piece of ribbon, sewing on the underside of the ribbon.

2 Turning the ends under, stitch one ribbon across each end of the pillow, 2 inches in from the side edge with the bead trim facing out. Decorate the central panel of the pillow with a selection of feathers, brooches, or trimmings. When you are happy with the design, sew them in place.

3 Cut the veiling or net to fit the central panel of the pillow cover. Lay it over the decorations and stitch it on neatly.

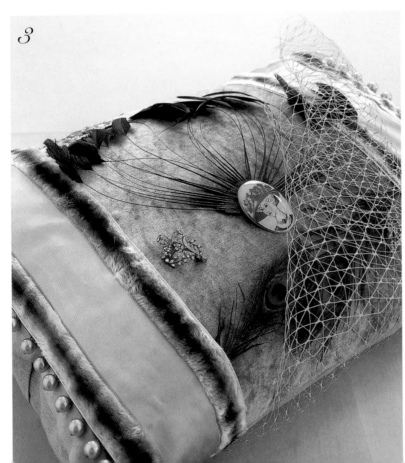

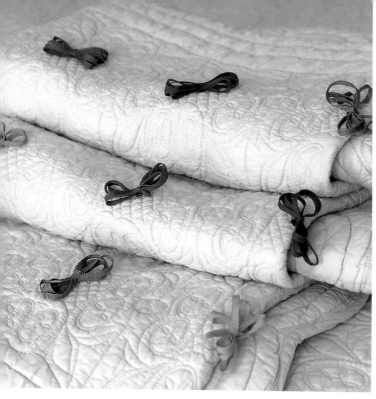

LEFT Little ribbon tufts in soft shades of taupe and blue decorate an otherwise plain pale blue bedspread for a fresh contemporary look. The tufts are made from looped ribbon, a ¼-inch-wide grosgrain (made of rayon, in this instance, so nicely floppy), attached with a couple of stitches through the center (see technique on page 40). Tufts can be made out of yarn, cord, or ribbon and are a really easy and versatile embellishment.

OPPOSITE Dress up your bed in crisp new white sheets customized with ribbons and trims. Sew a long satin fringe along the turn-down edge and follow this with a pretty rosebud trim. I didn't want the ensemble to match perfectly, so I used a mix of harmonizing colors—green, pink, and blue—and trimmed the pillowcases with different ribbons so they are not all the same. Don't skive from the ironing—when you slip into bed, you will be glad you made the effort.

BELOW A mixture of vintage organdy and velvet ribbons in exquisite jewel colors have been used to make a truly opulent bedspread. The ribbons, in different widths ranging from 2 inches to 4 inches, have been sewn onto the silk backing fabric in parallel lines. The organdy ribbon creates a shot effect over the silk, as the color of the fabric underneath shows through the ribbon's fine texture. Wide ruffle-edged ribbons in a contemporary palette were attached to the center of a couple of old scatter cushions to form a decorative band.

bed dressing As a child, I couldn't get to sleep until I had been tucked in under a crisp sheet, two satin-edged blankets, and a huge comforter. It often took my mother three tries to get it tight enough. All the beds in my house have blankets and sheets, with the turn-down edges at the top trimmed with ribbons. Once, for a photo shoot for a magazine, I attached a ribbon of dancing bears and flowers to my daughter's sheet using double-sided tape. It stayed in place for six years, even through hot washes. All washable ribbons are a great way to personalize sheets, pillowcases, duvet covers, or bedspreads. Jacquard woven ribbons are perfect and so versatile. They come in sophisticated stripes, gingham, Tyrolean styles, and children's motifs.

ribbon-covered coat hangers

How luxurious to have all your clothes hanging on beautiful trimmed hangers.
I would put them in a French armoire, the inside trimmed with fabric and the
doors edged with thin velvet ribbon in fuchsia, orange, and lime. Or use one to
display a gorgeous dress or vintage shawl as a sculptural piece in your bedroom
(see page 128). You only need lengths of 12 inches, so you can use up all your odd
pieces of ribbon and mix colors and textures—organdy, satin, and tweed, for
example, or leather, suede, and leopard print—and add beads, feathers, fringes,
pompoms, rosettes, and tassels. Either use purchased padded hangers or cover
standard wooden or plastic hangers with batting and muslin and decorate these.

1 Place the ribbons side by side on a soft board,
with the right sides facing down. You need a total
width of about 2½ inches more than the length of
the hanger. When you are happy with the design,
make sure the ribbons butt up to each other and
pin the ends. Cover with iron-on interfacing and
fuse according to the manufacturer's instructions.

2 Turn the fabric over so the right side of the
ribbons is facing up, then add other ribbons and
trims by layering them on top of the ribbon
fabric. Pin them in place, then neatly sew along
both edges to attach.

3 Pin the bead fringe to the underside of the
coat hanger in the center and sew.

4 Using the point of the scissors, make a small
hole in the center of the fabric. Pass the hook
of the coat hanger through the hole and wrap the

fabric around the hanger. Gather the open ends
of the fabric with a running stitch and pull into
shape around both ends of the hanger.

5 Fold in both long edges and pin then sew,
butting each one up to the central bead fringe.

MATERIALS

Padded coat hanger

Selection of ribbons, approximately 12 inches long

Soft board and pins

Iron-on interfacing and iron

Selection of trimmings

Needle and thread

Bead fringe, the length of the hanger and 1 inch deep

Pointed scissors

curtains & blinds

THIS PAGE These stunning curtains have been decorated with what I call "ribbon spiders," layered pieces of organdy and wire-edged ribbons stitched together and frayed. The bottom of the curtain has been trimmed with sumptuous organdy, taffeta, and georgette ribbons (see pages 118–19).

OPPOSITE All the fragments of chandelier glass that I have collected over the years have a small hole, so they are easy to wire to create a modern masterpiece—a lamp, perhaps (see page 145), or a "beaded" curtain, which can be hung at a window to project a light show onto the walls and floor, or used as a room divider, as here, which is like looking through icicles into a secret forest beyond. The drops used for these curtains are a mixture of shapes and sizes.

crystal curtains
to silk drapes

Ideas for windows are thrown wide open when it comes to ribbons. Like glamorous versions of the plastic-strip door hangings found in English fish and chips shops, vertical lengths of ribbons turn a window into a picture (see below and page 13). Strands of fine organdy in lots of different colors would make a beautiful type of sheer curtain, while blue-and-white gingham would be pretty in a child's room.

As an alternative to strips of ribbon, fill a window with chandelier glass wired into lengths and see the prismatic reflections dance on the wall when the sun shines through (see pages 69 and 115). Be inventive and customize plain curtains and blinds—attach pretty silk flower petals to net for a little girl's bedroom and finish with a border of layered ribbon, for example, or hang a straw beach mat trimmed with colorful cotton tape as a blind to make a Robinson Crusoe-style hideaway for a teenage boy; edge paper blinds with layers of beaded trim or make a unique design with rows of ribbons. Heavy curtains make interiors too dark—I like light to stream into a room through lightweight fabric trimmed to perfection. And there

is no excuse not to go over the top—I always encourage this—now that feather trims and bead fringes are available in lengths of 4–6 inches, making them ideal for creating a dramatic frayed, layered, or beaded bottom for a blind or curtain.

Think laterally, as unexpected fabrics can be surprisingly effective as window dressings—leather looks luxurious, sleek, and contemporary, while less extravagant felt is a quirky and fun choice (see page 125). Sequin fringe may seem an unsuitable material for a curtain trim, but, hanging in random vertical strips over a white cotton or gauze panel, it gives the effect of a cascading waterfall (see page 124). Experiment with cutting, fraying, and threading ribbons through fabric or other ribbons to create a unique look. I invented what I call "ribbon spiders," which make great decorations for curtains or blinds (see pages 114 and 118–19). As I never throw anything away, I cut up my ribbon scraps, trimmed off the selvage all around, frayed away happily, and then stitched several together in the center to make a pretty layered motif. When you fray shot ribbon, which is woven from two colors—blue warp threads and red weft threads, for example—you will achieve fantastic color combinations.

OPPOSITE The view through a glass door leading into a messy study is obscured by a curtain made from strands of pure silk ribbon. The floral design in brownish purple and gold was inspired by my 1840s' ribbon design documents.

THIS PAGE Whenever I am on the hunt for ideas, I look in antiques stores. One day I came across a superb collection of panels covered with folded and pleated vintage metallic braid. They were the inspiration for these curtains, made from linen sheets cut lengthwise into strips, with ribbons sewn on in simple interlocking diamonds and zigzags (see also page 24).

Old linen sheets can be used in lots of ways—the ones I use are from an old French hospital. Others, bearing the letters HMP, came from British prisons; the quality is fantastic and they dye very well in the washing machine. I stuck suede leaf-shaped motifs onto some and transformed others using three horizontal layers of grosgrain ribbon in lime green, plum, and a pink shade I think of as mushed raspberries and cream (the color of a dessert the English call "Eton mess"). Simple linen panels cut from such sheets can be transformed by vintage tapes or modern ribbons—ombré grosgrain in various shades of blue, for example (see right). Think of different designs and draw them on paper first, if necessary, then fold and manipulate the ribbon into these shapes and stitch them onto the panels.

Don't just stop at the curtains and neglect the poles they're hanging from. Vault your imagination upward and change them in any way possible—wrap the finials with ribbon or cord (see page 39), hang beaded cords from the poles, attach pansy heads to the valance, or cover it with a garland of shells. Even curtain rings can be painstakingly covered with a fine ⅛-inch-thick cord, glued and wound around and around. You could create a spectacular bold look if you covered each ring all the way along the pole with cord in different primary colors. In addition, consider covering door or window frames with ribbon, either glued in place or attached with double-sided tape.

Decorative tiebacks securing your curtains are the height of elegance and put the finishing touches to well-dressed windows. All sorts of materials can be used to make them, such as semiprecious stones or chandelier glass (see pages 7 and 120–1). Use ribbon to make roses (see page 22), then attach them to lengths of wide ribbon to gather up the skirts of your curtains. A simple cord tieback can be made using the knotting technique on pages 54–5, and giant tassels can be fashioned from string or cord (see pages 42–3).

tulle curtain with ribbon "spiders"

Made from organdy and wire-edged ribbons in various colors and widths, these decorative ribbon "spiders" look so delicate sewn onto the sheer silk tulle curtain at random intervals. The pieces of ribbon have been layered and sewn together, then the selvages cut off and the edges frayed all the way around. For a more robust look, there is no reason why you can't make "spiders" out of satin ribbon instead of fine organdy. Don't fray the edges, but rather cut them with pinking shears and sew them to a silk fabric, which could be on a pillow cover or bedspread as well as curtains.

MATERIALS

For each spider:

2¾ in of 2¾-in-wide organdy ribbon

2½ in of 2½-in-wide organdy ribbon

2 2½-in-long pieces of 2-in-wide organdy ribbon

2½ in of 1½-in-wide organdy ribbon

2½ in of 1-in-wide organdy ribbon

2½ in of 2-in-wide wire-edged ribbon

Scissors

Pins

Sewing machine and thread

For the border:

2 pieces of 4-in-wide wire-edged organdy ribbon

1 piece of 2¾-in-wide georgette ribbon

1 piece of ½-in-wide taffeta ribbon

1 For each "spider," cut seven pieces of ribbon in varying widths and colors (see left). Layer them with the longest piece at the bottom and the wire-edged ribbon in the middle and pin then sew together with 1 inch of zigzag stitch in the center. Cut off the selvages and fray by pulling threads away from the cut edges (see page 20).

2 Measure the bottom of the curtains and cut the four different ribbons to this length (see left). Lay them on top of each other, starting with the two pieces of organdy, then the georgette and taffeta. Align them along one edge and pin then sew them together along both edges of the taffeta.

3 Fray all the ribbons except the taffeta, then stitch the edging to the bottom edge of the curtain and sew on the ribbon spiders at regular intervals.

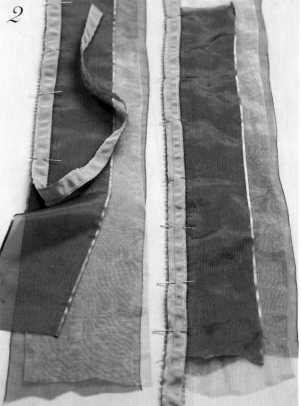

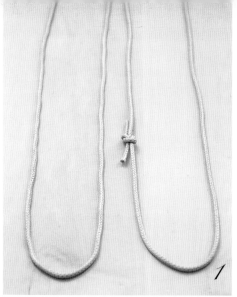
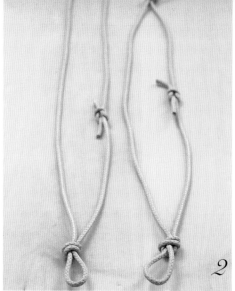

glass tieback

The rich colors of the curtain fabric—uncut taffeta ribbon—are visible through this tieback made from vintage glass. I found the stunning large pieces of glass in a French flea market. They were probably part of the central arm of an old chandelier—and what delight it gives me to see them used in this unconventional way. The rope part is covered with washed glass chips that were threaded onto a length of wire. The subtle color of this old dull glass enhances the vintage look—this tieback could have been in a French chateau for a hundred years.

MATERIALS
Approximately 2 yards of ⅜-inch-thick cord
Scissors
2¼ yards of wire or strong thread
Enough glass beads to cover 32 inches of cord
3 glass molds with large holes (NB: see step 6)

1 First, figure out how long your tieback needs to be—an average tieback is 32 inches. Cut a piece of cord twice that length, plus an extra ¾ inch to allow for the knots. Fold the cord in half and tie the ends together in a double square knot.

2 Move the square knot to the center of one long side and make a knot approximately ¾ inch from each end of the doubled cord. This will create a loop at each end for hanging up the tieback.

3 Thread the beads onto wire or thread. You can use a continuous length or several shorter ones.

4 Attach the loops to two hooks, so the cord is taut between them (either hammer two nails into a block of wood or hook the loops over two chair

backs). Take one end of the beaded wire or thread and secure it just below one of the knots by twisting it or knotting it around the cord. Then begin wrapping the beads around the cord.

5 Continue wrapping the beads tightly around the cord secure below the second knot, as before.

6 Finally, pass the glass molds to the center of the tieback. If they won't pass over the beads, you will need to wrap the cord part of the way, thread on the molds, and then continue wrapping.

THIS PAGE Layering trimmings is the key to creating impact, and I thought that using two different styles of bead fringe with a braid in between would really make these linen scrim curtains stand out. The linen itself is nondescript, but perfect for letting soft diffused light into the room; the beads glow as the natural light bounces off them. The bottom trim is sewn across the curtain so the 4-inch-deep bead fringe hangs just above the hem line. The ½-inch-wide braid is placed parallel to and about ¾ inch above the heading tape, with the 2-inch-deep bead fringe about 1¼ inches above. I would love to see this combination of trimmings used on the curtains of a four-poster bed, along the bottom of the drapes and on the heading.

1 Working on the right side of the shade, apply double-sided tape along both side edges. Starting at the bottom of one side, remove the backing and stick a piece of ribbon along the edge. Repeat on the other side of the shade.

2 Put double-sided tape along the bottom of the shade. Removing the backing as you work, stick on the feather trim, pressing the heading tape firmly.

ribbon- & feather-trimmed shade

A basic and functional paper shade has been reinvented with 2-inch-wide grosgrain ribbon in rich purple along both side edges and chic peacock-feather trim along the bottom. Both trimmings are attached very simply with lengths of double-sided tape. The shade still folds perfectly when pulled up, and, in fact, the ribbon edging gives the sides substance. The possibilities for creating different looks are endless: any ribbon could be used, such as a decorative jacquard print in an elaborate design, perhaps, with ostrich feathers or bead fringe in a harmonizing color along the bottom edge, or a jaunty gingham teamed with pompom fringe in primary colors. Here the purple of the ribbon sings out beside the blue-green of the peacock feathers.

LEFT The sequin fringe that has been sewn onto these sheer curtains in random lengths is made from very fine chain with a tiny sequin on every link. It cascades down the curtains like water or icicles, shooting light in all directions across the room. It is exceptional stuff and has hundreds of uses. The first that comes to mind is holiday decorating, but it is far too beautiful to see for only a few weeks a year. It could also be wound around a lampshade to great effect, as it would sparkle and glisten in the light.

OPPOSITE My memories of freezing winters in Cumbria with no central heating give me plenty of ideas for how to keep warm. This felt curtain is a colorful way to keep out the chilly drafts that whistle under the doors of old houses, and the bright colors look jolly on a winter's day. The two pieces of felt have been joined using fusible web, though they could just as easily be sewn. Slits were cut in the felt, and the striped grosgrain was slotted through and held in place with stitches at both ends. I chose this particular ribbon, the award-winning V V Rouleaux grosgrain, because it matches the "outside inside" bench on the right of the door, similar to the one on pages 96–7. You could create all manner of shapes depending on where you position the slits, including letters and numbers—your family name or house number, for example. Hold the curtain up with large clips, found in any hardware store, attached to a pole above the door. Make your inventions multitask and use the draft stopper as a bedspread. Felt has the advantage of not fraying, but another fabric could easily be used if you edge the slits for the ribbon with zigzag stitch, like large buttonholes—try cotton cheesecloth with satin threaded through the slits.

surfaces

THIS PAGE When you think of plaid in interiors, the image that usually springs to mind is traditional—Royal Stewart tartan in heavy red, green, and blue on the carpets, walls, and curtains of a Scottish hotel. This layered ribbon technique creates a more contemporary idea of a tartan wall, with an open pattern of overlapping squares of grosgrain and satin ribbon in widths of 4, 2¾, 2, 1½ and 1 inches in colors that intersect well—moss green, plum, gold, and magenta (see page 27). Make a statement on a large expanse of wall, such as a landing or one side of a hall, or try this idea on one wall of a bedroom in a masculine combination of burgundy, rust, and black with a touch of powder blue.

walls to floors

It is important, I think, not to treat living spaces as permanently fixed. This would be too boring. Your home is an expression of you and your life, so do not allow either to become stale. Keep your environment vibrant and alive by changing the color of the walls, adding trims or other embellishments, or by introducing decorative sculptures or displays to create a new focus of interest in the room.

I have recently moved, so this gave me a great opportunity to start decorating from scratch. All the walls in my old home were painted in colors inspired by nature. I love the color of pheasant eggs and ornamental hen eggs—a mixture of sage green overlaid with putty blue and covered with a light wash of yellow. This makes the walls glow in all lights. For my new home, I looked for color ideas in the V V Rouleaux shops, where there are 5,000 ribbons and trims to choose from. It is so much easier to see how walls, furniture, and furnishings of different colors will work together if you have a successful color

combination already presented to you in a single ribbon. My collection of 1840s' ribbon design documents is a fabulous reference for color and texture, and time after time a vintage ribbon will spark a whole scheme. The mix of textures in a single ribbon frequently amazes me—satin, velvet, and even a fur edge, in one case.

So, how was I going to redo my living room when all the furniture, cushions, pillows, lampshades, and miscellaneous bits and pieces were toned with a pheasant egg? As ever, I took inspiration from old ribbons and objects such as a beautiful antique sewing box (see page 8), which suggested the color for the walls. To create a formal look, the walls were painted with a faux-panel design. I then added my own form of paneling by attaching 7-inch-wide vintage ribbon vertically to the walls with double-sided tape (see page 130). These ribbons are old French designs and have faded to an ombré effect in a deep blue-purple color. If you can't find a wide ribbon in the right color for your walls, the same look can be achieved using several widths of narrower ribbon, either fused together and then applied to the wall or attached separately side by side (see page 28).

In the same room I used a metallic jacquard ribbon braid in three shades of gold to edge the fireplace, with a matching gold cord running along the top of the baseboards

OPPOSITE Different textures of ribbons can be used for a woven-ribbon panel to create very different styles. Organdy ribbon in shot orange and fuchsia is a great choice for a boudoir, complete with pretty covered hangers (see pages 112–13), while red and white gingham would be ideal for a child's room (see page 152). THIS PAGE The lower part of the wall in this masculine hall of fame, with its school photographs and military memorabilia, has been decorated with a panel of woven ribbon in two shades of green. It looks as if it has taken hours to create, but the technique is actually very simple and can be applied to doors, chests, or cupboard fronts as well as walls (see page 29). To finish the top edge, I have used double-sided tape to attach a wide taffeta stripe in colors that remind me of an old school tie—gray-blue and green with red, fuchsia, and black pinstripes.

and around the door frames (see page 131). As a finishing touch, I also used gold cord to cover the door knobs. These trims tied in beautifully with some French gilt chairs. How, then, to change and update the furniture to go with the newly decorated walls? Just add ribbon, of course! In fact, even carpets and rugs can be edged with heavy-duty hard-wearing grosgrain ribbon (see pages 138–9).

Another effective way to apply ribbons to walls and other flat surfaces is in the form of a woven panel (see opposite and right). Follow the technique on page 29, using any texture and color depending on the look you wish to create—harmonizing colors give a subtle effect, while dramatically contrasting ones make a bold statement. Choosing a fine ribbon, such as organdy, means the colors show through the layers as the ribbons are woven under and over each other, creating interesting depths of color and shade. Panels look especially chic running along a hall between baseboard and dado (chair) rail, but they can also be hung vertically or used to add decorative detail to doors, cupboard fronts, or tabletops. Alternatively, make a feature wall on a large landing or in a hall or bedroom by applying a selection of ribbons in a large-scale plaid-style pattern of open interlocking squares (see pages 126–7).

Whenever I come across an interesting object, I imagine it being used in several ways. I once fashioned an ornamental Chinese hat into a lampshade that incorporates fantastic shapes—flower buds and blooms, ornamental vases, and tassels—and casts a wonderful wash of light and pattern onto the wall. This is also how I assess a ribbon, cord, fringe, or braid, visualizing it used in different ways on walls, furniture, lamps, and all elements of interiors. Mirrors and picture frames provide great possibilities for trimming with feathers, ribbon, or cord. A mirror or frame can be transformed into a collector's piece by covering it with a jacquard ribbon, while bows, rosettes, and roses in all textures and colors make lovely decorations (see pages 136–7 for some ideas).

OPPOSITE When I am bored with the décor in my living room, I imagine what ribbons and trims I could use to transform the look. Here a beautiful vintage ribbon runs vertically down the walls, attached at intervals with double-sided tape at the top and bottom. The striped acetate ribbon, which has the texture of taffeta, has faded over the years so that the blue shades into mauve. The 7-inch-wide strips make a temporary solution for a room that was rather plain, and can easily be replaced when I fancy a change.

THIS PAGE I added detail to the fireplace by edging it with ½-inch-thick cord and 1½-inch-wide jacquard ribbon in different shades of gold. These can be attached with glue or double-sided tape. The inch-thick cord that I used along the baseboard and around the door frame also features several of shades of gold. The door knob is covered with two different cords, glued in place, and the light switch is hidden by a pretty rosette with a crystal center, made by gathering one edge of a ribbon and shaping it into a circle. The gold scheme has an old-fashioned French look that complements the antique chair covered with an old fringed tapestry. If your walls are a vibrant color, such as turquoise, use plain cords in bright red, yellow, and blue, and create a stripe along the baseboard. Experiment with jumbo cords or use bright red grosgrain around doors or shelves.

LEFT A dramatic-looking mirror can always spice up a room. These are reeves pheasant feathers, which come in lengths of a yard or more. The brown, gold, and black stripes have an *Out of Africa* feel, which inspired the whole color scheme for the room. The feathers look like a cross between zebra and leopard, with a half-moon marking with a touch of color like a tiger's eye—rust and orange with a hint of green. The elegant and flowing length of this feather enables you to shape a flowing wheel of dramatic proportions. The feathers were softened with hot steam and bent into shape (see page 66), then glued at intervals to the back of the mirror.

OPPOSITE What better way to keep your home alive than by changing the color of the walls or adding new decorative sculptures or displays? This room has a calm and rather plain color scheme, so I wanted to create a focal point with an unusual decorative shell arrangement. A wreath such as this can be made in a similar way to the swag on the following pages. When you are deciding where to position such a piece, consider if the area will enhance your display—a chimney breast is often a good location. The colors of shells are beautiful—pearly polished creams and taupe with dark brown spots, and sometimes hints of pink and the palest blue. These shades are accentuated by the shiny beige wire-edged ribbon and the luscious pale blue and chocolate-brown 2-inch-wide velvet ribbon woven among the shells.

shell swag

I used a selection of shells in a variety of shapes, which enable you to emulate the sweeping contours similar to a coving by Grinling Gibbons or the stucco motifs on the ceilings of a great historical house. In fact, following these designs is a good way to make sure that you work the shells into the best possible shape. I have incorporated two vintage tassel tiebacks to finish the ends of the swags. I love the old-fashioned color and texture of these against the pearly shells.

1 Cut a piece of chicken wire approximately 2¾ inches wide and 3 yards long and shape it into a swag or wreath shape with your hands.

2 Select a light cotton, voile, or silk for your fill-in fabric. A dull neutral shade is preferable, as this will not detract from or overpower the color of the shells. You will need a piece approximately 16 inches wide and 3¾ yards long. Attach this to the chicken wire with silver florist's wire.

3 Weave the wire-edged ribbon over the fabric-covered chicken wire and attach it with wire.

4 Attach a tassel to both ends of the swag, positioning the cord in a decorative way.

5 Plan the display by laying the shells out on a flat surface and arranging them in a configuration you like. Start by placing the best and largest shells in the center of the design and work out, mirroring the left side with the right. Wire the shells by rolling a piece of florist's wire into a circle at one end, then apply glue to the back or inside of the shell, and push the wire loop into the glue and allow to dry (see page 64).

6 Attach the shells to the swag by pushing the wires through the fabric—use scissors to make a small hole if necessary. Secure on the reverse of the chicken wire with a double twist. Continue along the chicken wire, filling it in with shells in your planned configuration.

MATERIALS

3 yards of chicken wire, 2¾ inches wide

Wire cutters

3¾ yards of cotton, voile, or silk fabric,
    16 inches wide

Florist's stub wire

4½ yards of 2¾-inch-wide wire-edged ribbon

2 decorative tassels with tieback cords

Mixture of shells in different shapes and sizes

Hot glue gun

RIGHT The frame of this mirror was beginning to look a bit battered and tired, so I covered it with a lovely combination of blue floral metallic jacquard ribbon, a small braid, brown printed mock leather, thin gold cord, and brown grosgrain ribbon, with a metallic furnishing trim finishing the outer edge. The width of the frame and its contours should inform your choice of ribbon—in this case, the jacquard ribbon is 1½ inches wide and fits its part of the frame exactly. These trims, simply glued in place, have transformed a plain frame into a stylish vintage collection piece.

OPPOSITE There are lots of textures of ribbon and different ways to manipulate them, though wire-edged ribbon will keep its shape best. You can ruche, pleat, fold, and layer more than one color; you can tie ribbons in simple bows or form them into flowers or rosettes. The decorations shown here, which illustrate a variety of techniques, complement each picture and together make a lovely gallery. The two rosettes on the bottom row have been made by the same technique as the green key adornment on page 23, one in a bold combination of turquoise and orange, and the other in rich brown grosgrain. The ruched circular rosette (top center) is like the one on pages 77 and 131. In a multiple display such as this, use a mix of ribbons and beads for centerpieces. I used an old metal component for the center of the olive-green wire-edged taffeta bow-rosette (top left), while the center of the luscious shot gray-blue wire-edged taffeta bow has been wrapped with a small piece of jacquard braid (top right).

BELOW, LEFT TO RIGHT Silver cord with wire incorporated inside it makes the perfect stand-up multiple bow for a picture; swathes of shot organdy ribbon have been ruched to form vibrant rosettes to decorate the top of a mirror (see the Ruching Ribbon with Thread technique on page 21); the wires of this wire-edged ribbon have been pulled on both sides to create a ruched pleated effect (see page 21), then the ribbon has been looped three times and secured in the center with a crystal stud.

LEFT Rugs and small mats can be edged easily and are perfect for beside the bed or bath, or in front of a fireplace. A heavy-duty braid, such as this grosgrain ribbon, requires a hot glue gun to attach it permanently, but double-sided tape can be used for an instant and more temporary new look. The colors of this stripe were inspired by the packaging of the clean bed linen when it was returned from the laundry to our home in the Lake District when I was a child.

OPPOSITE This ribbon, used as edging for a stair carpet, was inspired by horses' girths. The ribbon or webbing for girths is made in the same way as any other ribbon, cut into lengths and stitched with leather and buckles to attach it to the saddle. I have, over the years, been frustrated that no one was making a wide heavyweight grosgrain, as I could think of lots of uses for this type of ribbon. But I have found two manufacturers who will make special colors for me, and I find this very exciting. If you have a minimalist hall with plain cream carpet on the stairs, what better way to add color than with this black-and-red striped grosgrain attached with a hot glue gun? The center of the stair tread is trampled on much more frequently than the edges, so the ribbon will not get too worn. When it does, just choose a new design—for example, horizontal stripes in cream and turquoise intersected with vertical stripes of purple, moss green, mauve, and fine sky-blue pinstripes. Instant reinvention and stimulation for the senses as you climb the stairs.

THIS PAGE Wire-edged ribbon comes in hundreds of exciting colors, and I especially love the lush shades of green. Wrapped around a lampshade, the undulating layers of ribbon catch the light because of the shot effect of the green warp and blue weft threads (see pages 150–1).

OPPOSITE The fluorescent yellow lampshade and vibrant green stripe in the uncut-ribbon silk curtains look superb against the pale brown walls. The shade is covered with overlapping lengths of 2-inch-wide frayed wire-edged ribbon—the wire on one edge was cut off and the yarn pulled away to create a frayed edge ½ inch wide (see page 20). The ribbons were then glued top and bottom on the inside of the shade. The wreath is made from crystal chandelier pieces wired to a circular metal base.

lighting

pendants to table lamps

Ribbons, trims, braids, cords, feathers, glass beads, chandelier drops, and any other kind of decorative bits and pieces—what we call "components" at V V Rouleaux—can be used to transform a basic light design into a stunning focal point for any room. Wrapping and gluing or wiring and hanging these endless attachments will turn pendants, wall lights, table or floor lamps, and their shades into unique fixtures.

When you are planning the reinvention of a light fixture, lampshade or lamp base and are choosing what trimmings you will use, try to picture the end result in your mind's eye before you start. I have a clear image of how a lamp stand will look when covered with waxed cord, for instance, or I'll envisage a lampshade entwined with faux-glass beads or finished with frayed-ribbon roses in apple green with a hint of rose on the edge, with the same ribbon covering the whole shade. It is exciting and gratifying to try out a new idea and then have people say, "How marvelous! I would never have thought to do that." This is exactly what happened when I used parallel rows of black pompom braid around a lampshade (see page 146)—braid that is more usually seen around the bottom rim of a shade or along the edges of curtains

and pillows. Using different colors of this same trim—let's say, pink or lime green—would instantly change the design from chic and contemporary to fun and young, making it perfect for a girl's bedroom or children's study. Lamps create a warm atmosphere and can light up a corner of a room with more than just a bulb. An exquisite shade will still give you enough light to read by, but, as can be seen on page 149, a dramatic creation with wispy feathers along the top and bottom in subtle hues of deep green has such presence that it's like having a well-dressed and witty guest in the room.

Old lampshades in many different great shapes are easy to find in thrift shops and flea markets—and the bigger they are, the better for making an impact. This is your blank canvas for layering fluid yellow goose feathers above a base of multicolored beads, for example—see how that draws attention to itself (page 144), while draping a shade with bead fringes and tassels or bending beaded branches around it could not be easier (see

THIS PAGE I love using unusual materials for decorating lampshades. Here, branches of yellow faux glass were simply wound around the wire frame, starting at the top and working down so that it is evenly covered, with yellow and white faux-glass flowers attached at intervals. The effect is organic, as though a climbing plant with spectacular yellow blooms has grown over the shade. The dark plum deep-buttoned chair is from the era of Napoleon III and has a fantastic central panel of tapestry ribbon. OPPOSITE Waxed cord has so many uses, but its great texture makes it especially good for winding around objects of all shapes and sizes. This boring candelabra has been covered and wrapped in turquoise waxed cord, transforming it into a contemporary showpiece (see also page 146).

right and page 147). Secondhand stores are a treasure trove for sourcing basic materials such as antique fringes, old glass beads, and chandelier drops.

Of course, gorgeous, colorful ribbons really come into their own when it comes to creating the most elegant wrapped lampshades, whether wire-edged taffeta trimmed with ribbon roses (see pages 140 and 150–1), frayed-edged ribbon (see page 141), or woven ribbons in a stunning combination of shot organdy, thick red grosgrain, and brushed cotton (see page 146). The options for color and texture are as endless as the varieties of ribbon itself, and how you choose to employ them can be as traditional or as contemporary as required.

Another straightforward idea, and so easily achieved, is illustrated on pages 152–3—simply glue a selection of your favorite trims, ribbons, and bead fringes to a basic paper-globe shade. This inexpensive design can be implemented with an array of brightly colored and patterned trims to make it suitable and fun for a child's bedroom. However, if it is done with a silky black fringe, white fur, clear glass beads, and suede braid, all layered around the paper globe, it would be the perfect addition to a sophisticated living room or study furnished with black leather sofas and suede chairs.

Don't stop at shades—lamp bases are ripe for reinvention, too. If the base is a good shape, cover it by wrapping it in layers of cord, swathes of 2¾-inch-wide grosgrain ribbon, or lengths of wired beads. If the base does not have a particularly attractive shape, stand the lamp in a large glass container and fill to the brim with shells, beads, buttons, unfurled ribbon, spools of silk—you name it (see page 145).

All sorts of components can be used to adorn lights and I hope the following ideas will lead you to experiment with unusual objects that I haven't thought of. Anything that can be wired or threaded—glass beads, chandelier drops, feathered fringes, shells, fabric flowers, and sparkling paper butterflies—can be attached to any light that's in need of a revamp, as well as to those inexpensive paper globes that are widely available in various shapes, sizes, and colors.

OPPOSITE Lamp stands can become boring after a while or out of fashion, so I am always thinking up ways to change them. This lamp base was decorated with a selection of old glass beads, which come in loads of colors—red, yellow, blue, orange, black, clear—and in very random shapes. I threaded the multicolored beads onto a length of wire (see page 60–1) and attached it at the base with strong glue before wrapping the beaded wire closely around the base. This technique would look just as fun and contemporary on a cylindrical or shaped base, though you will need to glue the rows of beads as you go to prevent them from slipping off the curves. I wanted to make a real statement with the shade, so I wrapped it in layers of bright yellow goose-feather fringe, which I glued around the bottom edge first, before swirling it around and around until I reached the top and glued it around the rim to finish.

LEFT Wired chandelier glass can be put to work in transforming a plain shade. The strands have simply been wired around the top rim of the shade and draped over the sides so the light can shine through. Make sure you use a sturdy lamp with a heavy base to support the weight of the glass.

BELOW Different-shaped glass vases filled with a variety of shells can be used to great effect to transform basic lamp stands. Simply insert the stand into a suitable-sized glass vase of any shape and add a selection of shells. To make it more economical, fill the center of the vase with crumpled paper or inexpensive gravel and conceal this and the lamp base with shells. As an alternative decorative filling, try glass beads, crystal chandelier drops, feathers, or lengths of ribbon.

ABOVE You can create woven-ribbon lampshades with a contemporary or traditional feel by using ribbons of different textures and colors. This one is made of shot orange organdy, thick red grosgrain, and brushed cotton ribbons on self-adhesive board (see page 29). The board is cut to the shape of the lampshade, folded around it, and glued at the back, then the top and bottom edges are trimmed with ribbon for a neat finish.

RIGHT A great way to update a lampshade is to cover it with pompom fringe, usually used to trim curtains and pillows, glued in rows one above the other. The stand is also given a contemporary new look by covering it with ¼-inch-thick yellow waxed cord. Following the technique on page 39, lay the lamp on its side and secure one end of the cord to the edge of the base using a quick-dry hot glue gun. Wrap the cord around the lamp stand, turning the lamp and layering the cord tightly, gluing as you go. Make sure the glue is dry at each turn and the cord is secure. If you have to join two pieces of cord, make sure the ends meet so the join is nearly invisible.

OPPOSITE Components such as branches of acrylic beads and leaves can be used to transform lamps into pretty floral creations. The branches are made of wire and can be bent around a shade and wired to hold.

1

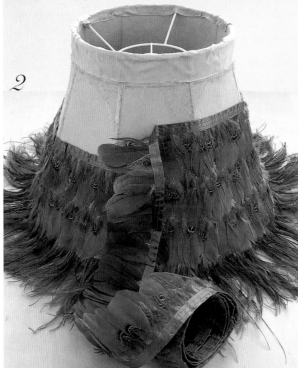

2

feathered lampshade

This fabulously decadent feathered lampshade is the star of one corner of my living room and is always a real talking point when people visit for evening drinks. The feathered fringe comes as a finished braid that is very easy to work with—simply swath it around an old shade, or even a hat. The fluffy feathers contrast dramatically with the old tin bin against the wall, while the many shades of green and blue work well with the sumptuous mix of contemporary textures—feathers, glass, satin, and the metallic gold tassel, all competing for attention.

MATERIALS

Lampshade, 12 inches tall,
    10-inch diameter (top) and
    16-inch diameter (bottom)
2½ yards of ostrich-feather
    fringe, 4 inches deep
    (1½ yards for the bottom edge
    and 1 yard for the top edge)
Tape measure
Scissors
Pins
Needle and thread
27 yards of turkey-feather fringe,
    2½ inches deep
Glue and glue gun

3

1 Measure the bottom edge of your lampshade and cut a length of ostrich-feather fringe to fit, adding ½ inch to overlap the ends. Pin the fringe around the bottom edge of the shade and then sew it to secure.

2 Glue a row of turkey-feather fringe above the ostrich-feather fringe, just touching it and hiding the heading tape. Continue building up rows of turkey-feather fringe, turning the lampshade as you work your way up its sides and gluing the fringe down in small sections.

3 When you reach the top rim of the lampshade, cut the turkey-feather fringe and glue the end down. Then attach a final row of ostrich-feather fringe around the rim, with the feathers pointing up, sewing it in place as before.

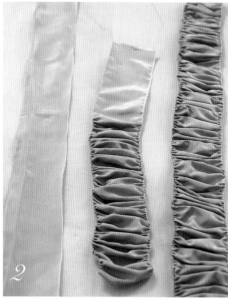

MATERIALS

Lampshade, 12 inches tall, 16-inch diameter

2-inch-wide wire-edged ribbon (50 yards for the
    lampshade and 2 yards for each rose)

2¾ yards bead fringe, 2½ inches deep

Scissors, glue, and glue gun

Pins, needle, and thread

1 Glue one end of the ribbon to the inside of the
top edge of the lampshade. Pass the ribbon over
the outside of the shade, then up the inside.
Continue in this way, overlapping the ribbon so
the shade is completely covered. Cut the ribbon
and glue the end on the inside of the shade.

2 Cut approximately 4½ yards of ribbon for the
ruching at the top of the lampshade and 6 yards
for the ruching at the base. Holding the ends of
the wire, ruche the ribbons (see page 21).

3 Adjust the ruched ribbons to fit around the
top and bottom of the lampshade by loosening or
tightening the wires. Pin to the shade and sew.

4 Pin the bead fringe to the inside of the bottom
edge of the shade. If it is a little thin, double
the trim to make it thicker as I have done here.
Secure with glue or sew in place.

5 To make a rose, cut 2 yards of ribbon. Pull the
wire on one edge only to form the gathers for the
flower. Then start rolling up the gathered wire
edge to form a bud. Keeping the gathered edge
in the same place, continue turning your bud to
create more tightly folded petals (see page 22).

6 Continue rolling, and as your flower gets
bigger, move the next fold outward, farther away
from the center. Adjust the flower shape as
necessary and pin in place as you go. Stitch to
hold, making sure you sew the center securely
so the bud stays in position and doesn't fall out
of the middle. Decide where you want to attach
the flowers and glue or sew them in place.

ruched ribbon & rose lampshade

Lampshades wrapped in wire-edged ribbon look glamorous in a living room or bedroom, and can be made in any color to blend or contrast with your interior scheme. Here 2-inch-wide two-tone ribbon in aqua and amethyst was used for the large lampshade and 1-inch-wide ribbon in bright green for the smaller shade. Make the roses as small and budlike or as large and blowsy as you like, and add as many as you wish to your lampshade, either around the bottom or top rim or positioned to one side.

trimmed paper-globe lampshade

I can't imagine why no one has done this before. This
type of lampshade makes the ideal blank canvas, and
although I love plain paper shades, they are much more
interesting when they are adorned with hundreds of
trims. Glue on all the scraps of ribbon and braid you
have been saving, even the bits you have kept from
when you were given flowers or presents. Long silky
and bead fringes hang down perfectly, while bead and
sequin tapes catch the light. The color scheme of this
room is based on the pair of old comforters on the bed.
These have been embellished with crochet rosettes,
pompom trims, and ribbons in the least prominent
colors in the fabric, which gives them a real lift. The door
panels are decorated with a weave of red velvet mixed with
red-and-white gingham and dotty ribbons (see page 29).
The storage box is the star of the room, covered in an
array of textures, including velvet, chenille, cotton, and
raffia, with a multicolored woven top (see page 87).

MATERIALS

Paper-globe lampshade, 16 in tall, 70 in circumference at widest point

2 yds of string

Pencil

Glue and glue gun

1¾ yd of ½-in-wide bead tape (for the central trim)

Above the central trim:

1¾ yds of ¼-in-wide flower tape

1½ yds of ½-in-wide flower tape

1⅜ yds of ½-in-wide woven tape

1 yd of ½-in-wide fur trim

½ yd of ½-in-wide faux-fur trim

Below the central trim:

1¾ yds of ½-in-wide lace

1⅜ yds of silky fringe, 2½ in deep

1 yd of ½-in-wide woven tape

14 in of silky fringe, 8 in deep

1 Assemble the paper lampshade by inserting the wire center according to the instructions. Find the center of the shade by wrapping a length of string around it, adjusting the position until it is around the widest point. You may find it helpful to place the shade on a vase or small box to prevent it from rolling around while you work. Mark the center point with a pencil and glue the central trim (the bead tape) around the shade at this point.

2 Attach the next trim parallel to the first at the desired distance from it. Make sure the two ends meet in the same place as before—this will be the back of the shade. Continue in this way, adding the rest of the trims and lining up all the seams at the same point at the back of the lampshade. Glue the last trim around the top edge, then glue the long silky fringe around the bottom edge.

3 Hang up the lampshade, making sure the seams are at the back.

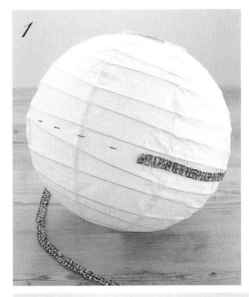

beaded-wire lampshade

Any decorative beads or drops can be used to create beautiful objects, as long as they have a hole by which to attach them. This easy lampshade has been made with a selection of pale green, pink, and clear faceted acrylic beads threaded onto lengths of silver wire with glass drops attached at the bottom. The heavy glass drops weigh down the strands and keep them straight. You can make the beaded strands as long as you wish—what about making them 6 feet long and hanging the light in the center of a spiral staircase? I love the way the light shimmers through these colored beads and makes them glisten, but you could use shells or wooden beads to produce a different look.

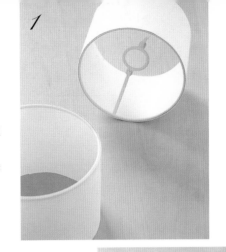

MATERIALS

Lampshade, 12 inches tall, 8-inch diameter

Tape measure and pencil

Scissors

1½ yards of 24-gauge silver wire

260 faceted acrylic beads, ½-inch diameter

20 pieces of card, 2 x 3 inches

Double-sided tape

Glue and glue gun

20 glass drops, 2¾ inches long

1 Measure the center point of the lampshade and mark it all the way around with a pencil. Cut the shade in half at this point.

2 Cut 20 pieces of wire 28 inches long and wire 12 acrylic or glass beads onto each, spacing them approximately 2 inches apart. To do this, thread on the first bead, hold it 2 inches from the end, then pass the wire around the bead and back through the hole. Twist the end of the wire around itself to secure. Leave a space of 2 inches and thread on the next bead, hold it in place and pass the wire around the bead and back through the hole, then pull the wire tight (see page 60). Continue until you have threaded 12 beads onto each wire and have 4 inches of wire left at the end. Make 20 beaded wires—or enough lengths to go around the circumference of the lampshade with approximately 1¼ inches between them. Wrap each wire around a piece of card to prevent the lengths from becoming tangled. Put double-sided tape around the inner bottom edge of the top half of the shade. Attach one end of the beaded wires to the tape, spacing them 1¼ inches apart.

3 Take the bottom half of the lampshade and cut slits 1½ inches deep all the way around the cut edge. Slot the bottom half of the shade inside the top half, making the slits a little deeper if you need to. This will enclose the ends of the beaded wires between the two halves of the shade. Finish with hot glue around the top of the wires.

4 Unravel the beaded wires and thread a glass drop onto the bottom of each to weight it down, with an acrylic bead on the end to hold it in place. Attach the bottom bead by bringing the end of the wire around the bead, as before, and twisting it just above it to secure.

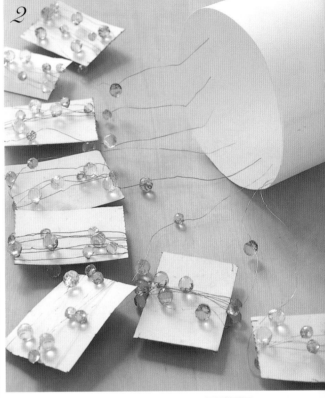

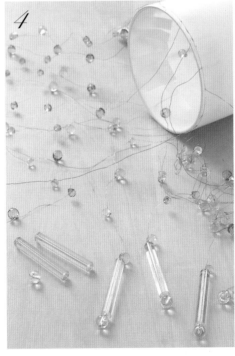

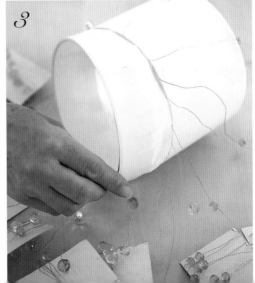

MATERIALS

Strong thread and scissors

Glass beads, ⅛ inch long

24-gauge silver wire

Selection of faceted and flower-shaped glass
    beads for tassel tops, in sizes ranging from
    ½ to 1 inch

1 For the central tassel, cut four pieces of thread
14 inches long and thread them with the ⅛-inch
beads. Cut a piece of wire 4¾ inches long and
secure all the ends of the beaded threads in the
center of this wire, making a double twist to hold.

2 Make three smaller tassels for the top of the
light fixture in a similar way, using two beaded
threads of 9 inches for each tassel. Wire each
set of two lengths into loops as before.

3 In addition to creating tassels, thread
different lengths of beads and fashion these into
loops, bows, and flowers—whatever shapes you
wish and as many as you need to adorn your light.
Just secure the loops with pieces of wire to hold
them in place, leaving enough wire to attach the
decorations to the light fixture. You can also
create more complicated motifs by joining
several shapes together, placing two or more on
top of each other and securing them with wire.

4 Embellish the top of each of the tassels by
wiring on a decorative loop or by threading on
a selection of larger faceted beads in different
shapes and sizes. Make the larger central tassel
the star of the piece.

5 Finally, attach the various beaded shapes
and tassels to the arms of the light, twisting the
ends of the wires securely around the metal
fixture and tucking them in neatly so they don't
show from the front.

glass-bead wall lights

Glass beads of all sizes can be used to embellish wall lights—larger crystal drops can be wired and hung from the lights (see page 57), while small beads can be threaded and made into tassels and other decorative adornments. I have used only clear glass beads with this traditional light fixture, but different color combinations could be used for a more contemporary design. Delicate beads like the ones used here work so well as they can be wired and then fashioned into pretty shapes. If you have any spare chandelier glass, or even a broken necklace, you can add these pieces to the tops of tassels.

suppliers

If you find yourself in the great cities of Europe, you'll want to visit these fantastic shops and boutiques for all the ribbons and trims you can carry! If you're at home or simply prefer to shop online, check out many of the stores' websites listed below.

ribbons & trims

V V ROULEAUX ATELIER & DESIGN
Head Office:
Trade Vaults, 6 Tun Yard,
Peardon Street,
London SW8 3HT
England
www.vvrouleaux.com

V V ROULEAUX is the leading ribbon and trimmings company in Europe, and their retail shops stock more than 5,000 different items, many of which are featured in this book. A specific selection of ribbons and trimmings available from the V V Rouleaux range, and illustrated on pages 16, 18, and 36, are listed below. To place an order, go to the company website where you will be guided through ordering, purchasing and shipping details.

basic ribbons (see page 16)

1 Single-sided velvet: code 10134 col 625
2 Double-sided velvet: code 17306 col 22
3 Plain taffeta: code 12384 col 5
4 Shot organdy: (code 11796 col 3
5 Grosgrain: code 12391 col blue
6 Picot satin: code 18071 col 821
7 Moire taffeta: code 13276 col 20
8 Wire-edged: code 7518 col 21
9 Jacquard wire-edged: code 12896 col 180
10 Organdy with satin edge: code 13255 col 20
11 Organdy with transfer dot print: code 13082 col 3
12 Satin: code 10124 col 11
13 Picot grosgrain: code 13704 col 55/115
14 Stretch organdy: code 12919 col 424
15 Metallic jacquard wire-edged: code 7730 col 7

special ribbons (see page 18)

1 Pleated satin: code 01521 col pink
2 Knitted wool braid with metallic thread: code 17144 col v2
3 Knitted braid: code 08462 col v1
4 Linen jacquard: code 17534 col 601
5 Pleated taffeta: code 11773 col c15
6 Woven jacquard with seersucker center: code 18711 col plum metallic
7 Organdy: code 12449 col 076
8 Denim stitch tape: code 15937 col 4
9 Lace: code 18162 col 51
10 Satin organdy stripe: code 17967 col 2
11 Vintage picot taffeta
12 Box-pleat stripe satin: code 18122 col 4
13 Llinen with jacquard design: code 8857 col brown
14 Pleated organdy: code 12678 col pink
15 Flower pom tape knitted and hand-stitched: code 18710 col pink yellow red
16 Transfer dot print grosgrain: code 13336 col 09
17 Taffeta with colored edge: code 10801 col 6
18 Hand-embroidered velvet: code 17742 col light blue

cords & trims (see page 36)

1 Silver metallic loop fringe: code 17296 col gray
2 Mock suede lace-cut tape: code 00474 col 60
3 Beaded glass trim: code 10659 clear
4 Mock snake leather: code 11534 col gray
5 Jacquard silver metallic braid: code 17370 col silver
6 Twisted metallic cord: code 17403 col green gold
7 Waxed cord: code 16595 col 15
8 Knitted braid: code 12330 col 825
9 Scroll gimp: code 07018 col 1603
10 Jute string: code 10134 col 625
11 Chenille cord: code 08432 col 3891
12 Suede tape: code 03644 col 59
13 Braided suede cord: code 00276 col 2
14 Twisted silky cord: code 07182 col 814
15 Jumbo silver metallic cord: code 8713 col silver
16 Waxed mock-leather cord: code 17714 col yellow
17 Twisted cord: code 16414 col 2
18 Metallic jacquard braid: code 17359 col silver black
19 Flange cord: code 10508 col 228
20 Braided flange cord: code 03937 col 20
21 Dyed jute garden string
22 Flat waxed cord: code 16604 col 12
23 Large sisal cord

antiques

B&T ANTIQUES
47 Ledbury Road, London W11 2AG
Tel: +44 (0)20 7229 7001
www.bntantiques.co.uk
Renowned for mirrored furniture.

JOSEPHINE RYAN ANTIQUES
63 Abbeville Road, London SW4 9JW
Tel: +44 (0)20 8675 3900
Tues to Sun 10am–6pm
www.josephineryanantiques.com
From huge dressers to elegant escritoires—all sourced in France.

beads & buttons

THE BRIGHTON BEAD SHOP
21 Sydney Street, Brighton BN1 4EN
Tel: +44 (0)1273 740 777
Mon to Sat 10am–5.30pm, Sunday Midday–5pm
www.beadsunlimited.co.uk
Phone for the catalog or order through the website.

THE BUTTON QUEEN
19 Marylebone Lane, London W1U 2NF
Tel: +44 (0)20 7935 1505
Mon to Wed 10am–5pm, Thurs and Fri 10am–6pm, Sat 10am–4pm
www.thebuttonqueen.co.uk
A family-run button box of a shop.

glass

PETER LAYTON, LONDON GLASSBLOWING
7 The Leather Market, Weston Street, London SE1 3ER
Tel: +44 (0)20 7403 2800
Mon to Fri 10am–5pm
www.londonglassblowing.co.uk
Peter Layton's studio produces blown glass, casting, and architectural work incorporating metals. There is also a gallery and lessons for beginners.

shells

EATON'S SEASHELLS LTD
Tel: +44 (0)1279 410284
www.eatonsseashells.co.uk
Mail-order company offering a wide selection of ornamental seashells.

fabrics

JAMES HARE SILK
PO Box 72, Monarch House, Queen Street, Leeds LS1 1LX
Tel: +44 (0)113 2431 204
www.jamesharesilks.co.uk
Suppliers of dressmaking and furnishing silks from around the world.

WHITCHURCH SILK MILL
28 Winchester Street, Whitchurch, Hampshire RG28 7AL
Tel: +44 (0)1256 892 065
Tues to Sun 9am–5pm
www.whitchurchsilkmill.org.uk
Silk has been woven here since the 1820s. They have a museum to visit as well as the working mill.

upholstery

CURTIS-GREEN
Unit 212, Avro House, Havelock Terrace, London SW8 4AS
Tel: +44 (0)20 7720 1123
www.curtis-green.co.uk
Michael Curtis-Green designs and builds his own range of fantastic bespoke furniture and upholsters whatever you might bring him.

JILL SAUNDERS
46 White Hart Lane, London SW13 0PZ
Tel: +44 (0) 20 8878 0400
They will do a beautiful job, or provide you with the means to do it yourself.

index

markets

CLIGNANCOURT MARKET, PARIS
The world's largest flea market—
"Les Puces"—at the Porte de
Clignancourt on the North side
of the Peripherique in Paris.
Sat 8.30am–6.30pm,
Sun 10am–6.30pm,
Mon 10.30am–5.30pm

**ALFIE'S ANTIQUES MARKET,
LONDON**
13–25 Church Street,
London NW8 8DT
Tel: +44 (0)20 7723 6066
www.alfiesantiques.com
Tues to Sat 10am–6pm
A huge selection of indoor traders
selling everything from objects to
vintage clothing, much frequented
by trade customers.

PORTOBELLO ROAD, LONDON
Portobello Road/Westbourne Grove,
London W11
Tel: +44 (0)20 7229 8354
www.portobelloroad.co.uk
Sat only 5.30am–5pm
On Fridays you'll find bric-a-brac at
the southern end and antique shops
abound on Westbourne Grove and
Ledbury Road.

retail

THE GENERAL TRADING COMPANY
2 Symonds Street, London SW3 2TJ
Tel: +44 (0)20 7730 5271
www.general-trading.co.uk

LAURA ASHLEY
Check the website for store details
Tel: +44 (0)871 9835 999
www.lauraashley.com

The publishers would like to thank **THE GENERAL TRADING COMPANY** for the kind loan of the following props: page 58 napkins; page 65 napkins; page 101 napkins, forks, knives; page 132 mirror.

The author would like to thank: Jill Kirkham at the Newcastle branch of V V Rouleaux, Kim Sissons, Cathy Alport, Claire Richardson, Jacqui Small, Kate John, Valerie Fong, and Zia Mattocks.